D0349132

000000695710

weekend projects

BABY CROCHET

weekend projects

BABY CROCHET

SUE WHITING

NEW
HOLLAND

This edition published in 2013 by
New Holland Publishers Pty Ltd
London • Sydney • Cape Town • Auckland

Garfield House, 86–88 Edgware Road, London W2 2EA, United Kingdom
Wembley Square, First Floor ,Solan Road, Gardens, Cape Town 8001, South Africa
1/66 Gibbes Street, Chatswood, NSW 2067, Australia
218 Lake Road, Northcote, Auckland, New Zealand

www.newhollandpublishers.com

A record of this book is held at the British Library and National Library of Australia

ISBN 9781780095110

Publisher: Fiona Schultz
Designer: Lorena Susak
Senior editor: Clare Sayer
Photographs: Sian Irvine and Paul Bricknell
Pattern checking: Sue Horan
Stitch diagrams: Kuo Kang Chen
Illustrations Carrie Hill
Production director: Olga Dementiev
Printer: Toppan Leefung Printing Limited
10 9 8 7 6 5 4 3 2 1

Keep up with New Holland Publishers on Facebook http://www.facebook.com/NewHollandPublishers

contents

introduction

Making something for a new arrival is both rewarding and fun. And, when you choose to crochet that special item, it can be quick too! Here you will find a lovely collection of easy designs to delight any new baby – or their parents, all of which can be completed in one or two weekends. All the patterns cater for tiny babies up to toddlers so you can make them for their bigger sister or brother too!

HOW TO CROCHET

It's not difficult to learn to crochet – especially if you are already a knitter and are familiar with handling yarn. Crochet only uses a hook and there is only ever one stitch on the hook at any time. This makes it much more versatile and greatly reduces the chances of dropping stitches! There are a few crochet stitches to learn but, as these are all variations on a theme, you'll find it really easy to master them. Once you've got the hang of one stitch, you'll pick up the others without difficulty.

WHAT YOU NEED

To crochet you need minimal equipment, just a pattern – you've got those in this book – and a few other items including yarn and a crochet hook.

Your pattern will tell you how much and what type of yarn you need to buy, and what size crochet hook to use. Crochet hooks come in lots of different sizes and there are different ways these sizes are measured – metric, imperial and American. Opposite is a chart that shows you the equivalent sizes in each measurement system.

Your pattern will also tell you if you need anything else – such as buttons or ribbon. Apart from these few things, there's not much else you need. A pair of scissors will be useful for cutting the yarn, and a tape measure will help you check the crocheted pieces are the right size. You will probably have to sew up a few seams, or darn in a few yarn ends – so you'll need a blunt-pointed needle with a large eye. Like those used for tapestry or sewing up knitted things, this sort of needle is not only easy to thread with a thick yarn but also the blunt 'point' slips between the strands of yarn and makes sewing up easy.

SIZING

All the designs in this book can be made for babies from newborn up to 18 months old. Although approximate ages are given, it's a much better idea to choose the size you want to make by measuring the actual chest size of the child. If you are still unsure what size to choose, compare the actual measurements of the garment – given at the start of the pattern – with those of something that fits the child well.

CROCHET HOOK CONVERSION CHART		
Metric	**Imperial (old UK)**	**USA**
2 mm	14	B1
2.25 mm	13	B1
2.5 mm	12	C2
3 mm	11	D3
3.25 mm	10	D3
3.5 mm	9	E4
3.75 mm	–	F5
4 mm	8	G6
4.5 mm	7	7
5 mm	6	H8
5.5 mm	5	I9
6 mm	4	J10
6.5 mm	3	K10½
7 mm	2	–
8 mm	0	L11
9 mm	00	M13
10 mm	000	N15

YARNS

Almost any knitting yarn can be used for crochet but, when making items for little ones, you need to bear a few things in mind. Children can be very fussy – and messy – and a baby's skin is delicate. Because of this, you'll find that a lot of the yarns featured in this book are machine washable. And they are soft too so they won't irritate baby's skin.

Colinette Jitterbug 100% merino wool, 291 m/318 yd per 110 g (4 oz) hank, machine washable (cold wool cycle), tumble dry (low setting).

Colinette Banyan 49% cotton, 51% viscose, 102 m/112 yd per 50 g (1¾ oz) hank, hand wash.

Colinette Prism 50% wool, 50% cotton, 120 m/131 yd per 100 g (3½ oz) hank, hand wash.

Rowan Cashsoft DK 57% extra fine merino, 33% microfibre, 10% cashmere, 130 m/142 yd per 50 g (1¾ oz) ball, machine washable (wool cycle).

Rowan Pure Wool DK 100% superwash wool, 125 m/137 yd per 50 g (1¾ oz) ball, machine washable (wool cycle).

Rowan Wool Cotton 50% merino wool, 50% cotton, 113 m/123 yd per 50 g (1¾ oz) ball, machine washable (wool cycle).

Rowan Handknit Cotton DK 100% cotton, 85 m/93 yd per 50 g (1¾ oz) ball, machine washable (wool cycle).

Rowan All Seasons Cotton 60% cotton, 40% acrylic microfibre, 90 m/98 yd per 50 g (1¾ oz) ball, machine washable (wool cycle).

Rowan Kid Classic 70% lambswool, 26% kid mohair, 4% nylon, 140 m/153 yd per 50 g (1¾ oz) ball, hand wash.

Rowan Kidsilk Haze 70% superkid mohair, 30% silk, 210 m/229 yd per 25 g (1 oz) ball, hand wash.

Rowan Cocoon 80% merino wool, 20% kid mohair, 115 m/126 yd per 100 g (3½ oz) ball, hand wash.

Rowan Big Wool 100% merino wool, 80 m/87 yd per 100 g (3½ oz) ball, hand wash.

Twilleys Freedom Spirit 100% wool, 120 m/131 yd per 50 g (1¾ oz) ball, hand wash.

ABBREVIATIONS

All crochet patterns are written in a sort of shorthand – all the 'technical' terms are shortened, or abbreviated, to just a few letters. These abbreviations are standard to almost all crochet patterns and here you've got a full list of all the ones you need for the designs in this book. Sometimes there will be a special stitch, or stitch group, used for one particular design only – if this is the case that special abbreviation will appear with the pattern it's needed for.

TENSION

The size of a finished piece of crochet is controlled by how big, or small, the stitches and rows are, and the term used to describe this is the 'tension'. Because the tension governs the size of the finished item and the amount of yarn you will need, it's really important you crochet at the correct tension.

To check your tension, make a small square of crochet in the stitch used for the garment, using the yarn and the size of hook given in the pattern. Make sure this tension swatch is at least 15 cm (6 in) square so that you can easily count the number of stitches and rows on it.

Once you've completed the crochet square, mark out with pins the number of stitches the tension section of the pattern states there should be to 10 cm (4 in). Measure the distance between the pins – if this measurement is 10 cm (4 in) your tension is correct and you are safe to make the garment using that size crochet hook.

If the distance between the pins is less than 10 cm (4 in), you are crocheting too tight and you need to make another swatch using a bigger crochet hook. And if the measurement is more than it should be, your crochet is too loose and you will need to use a smaller hook.

Check your row tension is correct in the same way. Once you've worked out what size hook you need to use, use this size of hook for the garment instead of the size stated in the pattern. If other sizes of hook are needed, you'll need to adjust the size you use here too – if you've used one size smaller hook to get the tension required, use one size smaller hook than stated for all the other hooks you need too.

FOLLOWING A PATTERN

All the garments in this book are in more than one size, and the different figures needed for each size are given as a string of figures inside square brackets [ ]. Where only one set of figures is given, this refers to all sizes.

The information inside the round brackets ( ) should be repeated the number of times given after the brackets.

The amount of yarn the pattern says you will need is based on an average requirement and if you alter the length you may need more or less yarn. Each pattern has been designed to work in the yarn stated – and it may not work correctly if any other yarn is used.

The pattern gives details of the order in which you should crochet the different pieces that go together to make up

CROCHET ABBREVIATIONS
alt – alternate
beg – beginning
ch – chain
cont – continue
dc – double crochet
dc2tog – (insert hook as indicated, yoh and draw loop through) twice, yoh and draw through all 3 loops on hook
dec – decreas(e)(ing)
dtr – double treble
foll – following
htr – half treble
inc – increas(e)(ing)
patt – pattern
rem – remain(ing)
rep – repeat
RS – right side
sp(s) – space(s)
ss – slip stitch
st(s) – stitch(es)
tr – treble
tr2tog – (yoh and insert hook as indicated, yoh and draw loop through, yoh and draw through 2 loops) twice, yoh and draw through all 3 loops on hook
yoh – yarn over hook
WS – wrong side
0 – no sts, times or rows to be worked for this size
cm – centimetres
in – inches
mm – millimetres

the completed item. This order should be followed as often a later piece will need you to refer back to the size of a previous section, or some pieces need to have already been completed in order to add an edging or band.

COMPLETING THE GARMENT

Once all the main pieces have been crocheted, the garment can be sewn together. It's often a good idea to press the sections first. This is much easier to do before they are sewn up – especially with small pieces like those that make up a baby garment. You should find all the information you need to press the pieces on the ball band but, if in any doubt, it is usually safe to press the pieces carefully on the wrong side using a warm iron and covering the work with a damp cloth. However, if you are using a totally synthetic yarn, use a cool iron and a dry cloth! Allow all the pieces to cool down and dry naturally before sewing them together.

With each pattern in this book there is a little diagram that shows you the shape each main crocheted piece should be when it is completed. Use these as a guide to what shape your work should be once pressed.

The crocheted pieces can be joined together in three ways – by back stitching the seams, over sewing the seams or by crocheting the edges together. Whatever type of seam you decide to work, use the same yarn for the seam as used for the crochet and, in the case of sewn seams, a blunt-pointed sewing-up needle.

Back stitching a seam

This type of seam gives quite a bulky seam on the inside of the garment but can be useful if the edge isn't totally straight, or to join shoulder seams.

To back stitch a seam, hold the two edges to be joined right sides together and work a line of back stitch as close to the edge as you can, working each stitch through both layers of the crochet.

Over sewing a seam

This gives a totally flat seam and it's a good idea to use this type of seam to join side and sleeve seams.

To over sew a seam, hold the 2 edges to be joined with their right sides together and simply over sew along the edge, working each stitch through both layers. Once the seam is complete and the sections are opened out, you should find this type of seam is virtually invisible and almost totally flat.

Crocheting a seam

This type of seam is a good choice for seams like shoulder seams as it is as elastic as the crochet is and will not split when the garment is put on or taken off.

To crochet a seam, hold the two edges to be joined with their right sides together and attach the yarn at one end of the seam. Using the same size crochet hook as used for the main sections, work a row of double crochet along the edge, working each stitch through both layers.

If there are any buttons, ribbons or trims to be added to a garment it is very important these are very securely attached so there is no risk of them coming off. Babies and toddlers suck everything, and put anything they can in their mouths, and they could easily choke on a button!

THE CROCHET STITCHES

Crochet is very simple and basically consists of just a few different types of stitch.

Starting the work

Before you start any crochet, you need to make your first stitch. To make this first stitch, make a slip knot by forming the yarn end into a loop and hooking the ball end of the yarn through this loop (**fig. A**).

Gently pull on the free end of the yarn (not the end leading to the ball) to tighten this first stitch around the body of the hook. You are now ready to make the next lot of stitches. All the following stitches should be worked using the length of yarn that leads to the ball, leaving the free (cut) end of the yarn to be used to sew a seam later if required (**fig. B**).

FIGURE A **FIGURE B**

Chain (ch)

A crochet chain is often used as the base for all the following stitches but it can also be used within a stitch pattern.

FIGURE C

To make a chain stitch, take the yarn end that leads to the ball over the crochet hook, wrapping it over, in front and under the hook. Now draw this loop through the loop on the hook to make the chain stitch (fig. C). Continue in this way until the required number of chain stitches have been completed.

Double crochet (dc)

This is possibly the most basic of crochet stitches.

To make a double crochet, insert the hook into the work. Wrap the yarn around the hook in the same way as for a chain stitch. Draw this new loop through the work – you should now have 2 loops on the hook (fig. D). Wrap the yarn around the hook again and draw this new loop through both the loops on the hook to complete the stitch (fig. E).

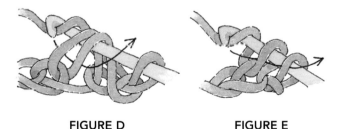

FIGURE D   **FIGURE E**

Treble (tr)

This is the other most commonly used crochet stitch. It's taller than a double crochet and therefore the work will grow faster if it's made up of treble stitches.

To make a treble, start by wrapping the yarn around the hook before inserting it into the work (fig. F). Wrap the yarn around the hook again and draw this new loop through just the work, leaving 3 loops on the hook. Now wrap the yarn around the hook again (fig. G). Draw this new loop through just the first 2 loops on the hook. There are now just 2 loops left on the hook. Wrap the

yarn around the hook once more (fig. H). Draw this new loop through both of the loops on the hook to complete the treble (fig. J).

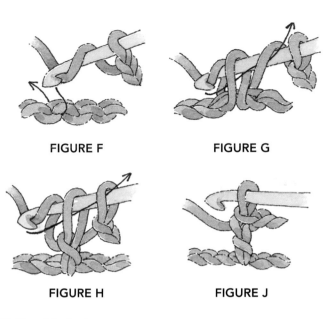

FIGURE F   **FIGURE G**

FIGURE H   **FIGURE J**

Half treble (htr)

This type of stitch is taller than a double crochet but shorter than a treble and it's made in a similar way to a treble.

To make a half treble, wrap the yarn around the hook and insert it into the work. Wrap the yarn around the hook again and draw this new loop through the work, leaving 3 loops on the hook (fig. K). Wrap the yarn around the hook again but this time draw this new loop through all 3 loops on the hook to complete the half treble (fig. L).

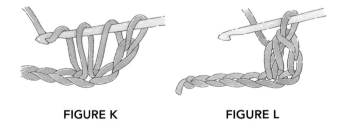

FIGURE K   **FIGURE L**

Double treble (dtr)

This stitch is taller than a treble. To make a double treble, wrap the yarn twice around the hook before inserting it into the work. Wrap the yarn around the hook and draw this new loop through the work, leaving 4 loops on the hook. Wrap the yarn around the hook again. Draw this new loop through just the first 2 loops on the hook. There are now 3 loops left on the hook. Wrap the yarn around the hook once more. Draw this new loop through just the first 2 loops on the hook. There are now 2 loops on the hook. Wrap the yarn around the hook again. Draw this new loop through both of the loops on the hook to complete the double treble.

Taller stitches

Stitches that are taller than a double treble can be worked in a similar way. For a triple treble (ttr), wrap the yarn around the hook 3 times before inserting it into the work. Wrap the yarn around the hook and draw this new loop through the work. *Now wrap the yarn around the hook again and draw the new loop through just the first 2 loops on the hook. Repeat from * until there is only one loop left on the hook – the triple treble is now completed.

   Bigger trebles can also be made in this way – for each extra bit of height to the stitch, wrap the yarn around the hook once more before inserting it into the work (4 times for a qtr). Complete each bigger stitch in the same way – by drawing each new loop through just the first 2 loops on the hook until only one loop remains.

Slip stitch (ss)

Often used to join sections or to move the crochet hook to another point to work the next set of stitches.

FIGURE M

FIGURE N

To make a slip stitch, insert the hook into the work. Wrap the yarn around the hook and draw this new loop through both the work and the loop on the hook to complete the slip stitch (**figs. M and N**).

PLACING THE STITCHES

Different crochet stitch patterns are often made up of the same sort of stitches but where these stitches are placed can alter the effect they create.

Working into the top of stitches

This is the standard way to place the next set of stitches and, unless a pattern says otherwise, this is how all the stitches should be worked.

   Across the top of each crochet stitch is a little 'V' formed by the yarn. Insert the hook through the work so that it slides under both of the bars that make up this 'V' (**fig. O**).

FIGURE O

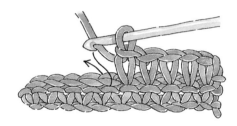

Working into chain stitches

As with all other crochet stitches, a chain stitch has a 'V' of yarn on one side, with a third bar of yarn running across the back.

   When working into a chain stitch, insert the hook through the centre of the 'V', picking up the underneath bar at the same time. This leaves just the front bar of the 'V' not enclosed in the stitch (**fig. P**).

FIGURE P

Working into the front (or back) of a stitch

By picking up just the front (or back) bar of the 'V' different effects can be created.

To work into the front loop (or bar) only, insert the hook through the work by sliding it under just the front bar that forms the 'V', and thereby picking and enclosing just one strand of yarn in the stitch. The remaining bar of yarn that formed the 'V' will sit on the surface of the work, forming a neat line across it (fig. Q).

FIGURE Q

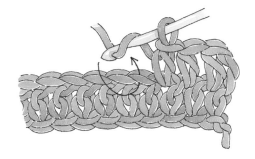

Working into the back loops (or bars) only in the same way will leave a line across the opposite side of the work (fig. R).

FIGURE R

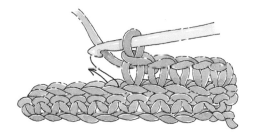

Working between stitches

Rather than working a new stitch into the top of the existing stitches, a new stitch can be worked between the stitches of the previous row. Obviously this is a lot easier to do if the previous stitches were tall stitches and it's easy to see where one stitch ends and the next stitch begins!

To work a stitch between the stitches of the previous row, simply insert the hook through the work between the 'stalks' that make up the previous stitches. Working stitches in this way means you are not adding as much height to the work as you would if you were working into

the top of them, and you are enclosing the strands of yarn that join the two stitches in this new stitch (fig S).

FIGURE S

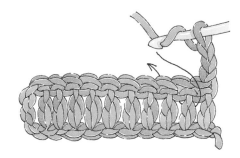

Working into chain spaces

A stitch pattern that is made of up lengths of chain between other crochet stitches will have what is termed a chain space (ch sp) underneath the length of chain stitches. To work into a chain space, simply insert the hook through this 'hole' before wrapping the yarn around the hook to make the new stitch (fig. T).

FIGURE T

MAKING FABRICS

Crochet stitches can be joined together to make a crochet fabric in two ways – in rows, or in rounds.

Working in rows

Working backwards and forwards in rows of crochet stitches that all sit neatly on top of each other forms a flat fabric. Each row of new stitches is worked from the right towards the left. At the end of the row, the work is turned and the next row of stitches is again worked from right to left. At the beginning of each row, the working loop, and the hook, needs to be raised up to the height of the stitches that are to be used for this new row. To do this, a short length of chain – known as a turning chain – is made. The length of this chain varies depending on the type of stitch being worked. Sometimes this length of chain will take the place of the first stitch of the new row, sometimes it won't – but your pattern should tell you whether it does or not. If the turning chain does count as the first stitch of the row, you must work into the top chain stitch when working back across the stitches so that no accidental decreases are made and the number of stitches remains constant (**fig. V**).

FIGURE V

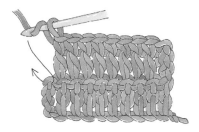

Working in rounds

As there is only ever one crochet stitch on the hook at any one time, it's really easy to work circular pieces of crochet by working round and round the work, instead of in rows. These circular pieces of crochet can form flat disks or tubes. Each new round of crochet is worked in the same sort of way as each new row of crochet, and at the beginning of each round there will be the turning chain. But, to join the end of each round to the beginning of it – and thereby form a tube or flat disk – the last stitch needs to be joined to the first stitch. Once all the stitches of the new round are complete, the ends are usually joined by working a slip stitch into the top of the turning chain (**fig. W**). When working in rounds of crochet there is no real need to turn the work at the end of each round. However, as crochet stitches look different on one side to the other, sometimes a pattern will tell you to turn the work after each round so that the required effect is created. If the pattern says 'turn', then you should. If it doesn't, then don't!

FIGURE W

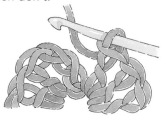

FASTENING OFF

Once a crochet section is completed, there will still be the one working loop – or stitch – on the hook.

To permanently fasten off this last stitch, cut the yarn about 10–12 cm (4–5 in) from the work. Take the yarn around the hook in the usual way and draw this cut end of yarn through the last stitch. Pull gently on the cut end to tighten the last stitch. Depending on how the pieces are to be joined together, cut the yarn so that a long end is left as this can be used to sew the seams.

SHAPING IN CROCHET

Obviously not all garments are made up of straight pieces of crochet, or shapeless tubes! So, at some point, you may need to increase or decreases stitches to make the piece the shape it should be.

There are lots of different ways this shaping can be worked and each method is more suited to one stitch pattern or shape than another. The patterns in this book will explain the way each piece should be shaped to achieve the desired end result.

WORKING WITH MORE THAN ONE COLOUR

The loop actually on the hook before a stitch is worked forms part of the new stitch. Therefore, if more than one colour is being used, you need to change to the new colour to complete the last 'yarn over hook and draw this loop through' stage. This will avoid messy lines where the two colours meet.

FANCY STITCH PATTERNS AND GROUPS

The basic crochet stitches can be grouped together or placed within the work to make a myriad of different effects. Whatever the effect created, each individual stitch will be worked in the way it would be normally – it is how it is placed within the work that creates the stitch pattern.

Sometimes one or more basic stitches are combined to create a special effect or type of stitch. If this is the case, you will find that a special abbreviation is used for this group of stitches, and how this group of stitches should be worked will be explained in the 'abbreviations' section of the pattern. Before you start your crochet, it's a good idea to read this section and practise the stitch group so that you know exactly what you are meant to do.

ADDING EDGINGS AND BANDS

Once the main crocheted pieces have been worked and any seams joined, you'll often find that edgings or bands are often worked to complete the item.

To work the edging, start by attaching the yarn at the point the pattern tells you to. Attach the yarn by making a slip knot on the hook and then working a slip stitch at the required position. Complete the edging following the instructions given with the pattern.

Edgings have a tendency to stretch as they are worked – but they are generally needed to hold an edge to a particular length. It's therefore a good idea to work the first round (or row) of any edging a little too tightly. That way, as any further rounds (or rows) are worked, it will gently ease itself out to the correct length.

There are no real hard and fast rules as to exactly how many stitches you need to work along an edge – it's a bit of a trial and error process! If in doubt, work too few stitches – especially if the edging is only one or two rounds (or rows). This can gently be stretched to the right length once you've finished. If, once you've completed your edging, it looks wavy or frilly, unpick it and start again! No matter how many stitches you work, try to space them out evenly along the edge and try not to split the yarn of the existing stitches as you insert the hook into the work.

Crab stitch

This is a version of double crochet and is quite often worked as the last round (or row) of an edging as it creates a neat 'beaded' finish that looks virtually the same on both sides.

Almost all crochet stitches are worked from right to left – but crab stitch is different. It is basically just a row of double crochet stitches that are worked the 'wrong' way around – from left to right. It can be quite tricky to get the hang of but, once mastered, it gives an attractive finish. To work a crab stitch edging, do NOT turn at the end of the last row (or round) – you are going to be working back along the stitches you've just made. Insert the hook from front to back under the two bars of yarn sitting across the top of next stitch to the right. Take the yarn under the hook and draw this new loop of yarn through the work. Wrap the yarn around the hook in the usual way and draw this new loop through both

loops on the hook – exactly as you would for any double crochet stitch. Now insert the hook into the next stitch to the right again, twisting the hook toward you and toward the right as you insert it. Take the yarn under the hook and draw this new loop through the work. Wrap the yarn around the hook again, taking it from the back, over, round and under the hook, and draw this new loop through both loops on the hook. Continue along the edge in this way. As each stitch is made it will form a little knot along the edge of the work. Crab stitch can stretch the edge it's worked along, so make sure the edge is quite 'tight' before you start.

CROCHET STITCH DIAGRAMS

Crochet stitch patterns can also be shown as diagrams. These show you exactly how each new set of stitches sits within the work in relation to the previous and next sets of stitches. Each pattern in this book gives you written details of exactly how to work each stitch pattern for each size and piece being made – but you'll also find a diagram that shows the basic stitch pattern. Use this as a visual guide, referring to the written pattern for how many stitches to actually work.

On these stitch diagrams, a different symbol is used for each type of crochet stitch. Below is a list of what these symbols mean.

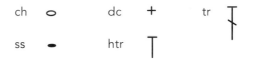

AFTERCARE

Once your garment is complete, it's a good idea to keep one of the ball bands. This will give you details of exactly how the yarn should be washed. If two yarns are combined within one garment, it should be washed to suit the more delicate yarn. For example, if one yarn is only suitable for hand washing while the other can be machine washed, the completed garment must be hand washed.

The Patterns

ARAN-STYLE JACKET

This cosy zip-up jacket features panels of textured diamonds and bobbles, on a base of simple double crochet, which echo traditional aran style knitting – but are surprisingly simple to achieve. Worked in a soft cotton and microfibre mixture yarn, the neat collar completes the look.

MEASUREMENTS					
age (months)	0–3	3–6	6–12	12–18	
chest	41	46	51	56	cm
	16	18	20	22	in
actual chest	47	52	58	64	cm
	18½	20½	22¾	25	in
length	22	26	30	34	cm
	8½	10¼	11¾	13¼	in
sleeve seam	13	16	20	26	cm
	5	6¼	7¾	10¼	in

MATERIALS
- 3 [4:4:5] x 50 g balls of DK in cream
- 3 mm and 3.5 mm crochet hooks
- Open-ended zip to fit

ABBREVIATIONS
- **rbtr** – work tr round stem of next st, inserting hook from right to left and from back to front
- **rftr** – work tr round stem of next st, inserting hook from right to left and from front to back
- **htr3tog** – (yoh and insert hook as indicated, yoh and draw loop through) 3 times, yoh and draw through all 7 loops on hook.

See also page 9.

TENSION
21 stitches and 20 rows to 10 cm (4 in) measured over pattern using 3.5 mm hook.
Change hook size if necessary to obtain this tension.

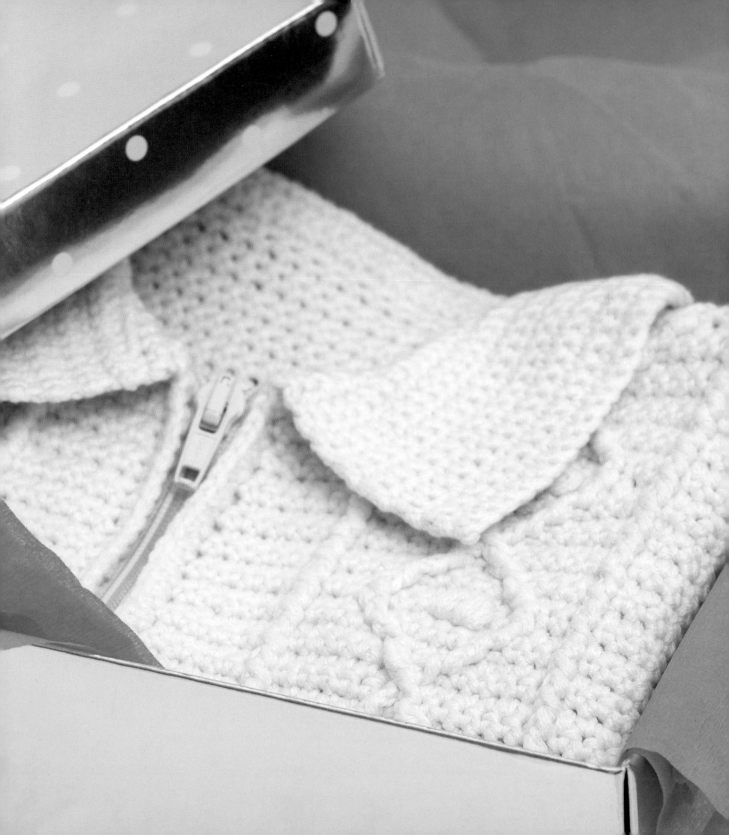

Pattern panel (16 sts)

1st row (RS): 1 rftr around stem of next st, 1 dc into each of next 6 sts, miss 1 st, 1 rftr around stem of next st, 1 rftr around stem of st just missed and keeping hook in front of rftr just worked, 1 dc into each of next 6 sts (there should be the tops of 2 sts missed between the sets of dc each side of the crossed relief sts), 1 rftr around stem of next st.

2nd row: 1 rbtr around stem of next st, 1 dc into each of next 5 sts, miss 1 st, (1 rbtr around stem and 1 dc into top) of next st, (1 dc into top and 1 rbtr around stem) of next st, miss 1 st, 1 dc into each of next 5 sts, 1 rbtr around stem of next st.

3rd row: 1 rftr around stem of next st, 1 dc into each of next 4 sts, miss 1 st, (1 rftr around stem and 1 dc into top) of next st, 1 dc into each of next 2 sts, miss 1 st, (1 dc into top and 1 rftr around stem) of next st, 1 dc into each of next 4 sts, 1 rftr around stem of next st.

4th row: 1 rbtr around stem of next st, 1 dc into each of next 3 sts, miss 1 st, (1 rbtr around stem and 1 dc into top) of next st, 1 dc into each of next 4 sts, (1 dc into top and 1 rbtr around stem) of next st, miss 1 st, 1 dc into each of next 3 sts, 1 rbtr around stem of next st.

5th row: 1 rftr around stem of next st, 1 dc into each of next 2 sts, miss 1 st, (1 rftr around stem and 1 dc into top) of next st, 1 dc into each of next 6 sts, miss 1 st, (1 dc into top and 1 rftr around stem) of next st, 1 dc into each of next 2 sts, 1 rftr around stem of next st.

STITCH DIAGRAM

KEY

+ dc

htr3tog

rbtr

rftr

6th row: 1 rbtr around stem of next st, 1 dc into each of next 2 sts, 1 rbtr around stem of next st, 1 dc into each of next 3 sts, (htr3tog into next st) twice, 1 dc into each of next 3 sts, 1 rbtr around stem of next st, 1 dc into each of next 2 sts, 1 rbtr around stem of next st.

7th row: 1 rftr around stem of next st, 1 dc into each of next 2 sts, (1 dc into top and 1 rftr around stem) of next st, miss 1 st, 1 dc into each of next 6 sts, miss 1 st, (1 rftr around stem and 1 dc into top) of next st, 1 dc into each of next 2 sts, 1 rftr around stem of next st.

8th row: 1 rbtr around stem of next st, 1 dc into each of next 3 sts, (1 dc into top and 1 rbtr around stem) of next st, miss 1 st, 1 dc into each of next 4 sts, miss 1 st, (1 rbtr around stem and 1 dc into top) of next st, 1 dc into each of next 3 sts, 1 rbtr around stem of next st.

9th row: 1 rftr around stem of next st, 1 dc into each of next 4 sts, (1 dc into top and 1 rftr around stem) of next st, miss 1 st, 1 dc into each of next 2 sts, miss 1 st, (1 rftr around stem and 1 dc into top) of next st, 1 dc into each of next 4 sts, 1 rftr around stem of next st.

10th row: 1 rbtr around stem of next st, 1 dc into each of next 5 sts, (1 dc into top and 1 rbtr around stem) of next st, miss 2 sts, (1 rbtr around stem and 1 dc into top) of next st, 1 dc into each of next 5 sts, 1 rbtr around stem of next st.
These 10 rows form patt panel.

Body

(worked in one piece to armholes)
With 3 mm hook, make 94 [106:118:130] ch.

1st row (RS): 1 dc into 2nd ch from hook, 1 dc into each ch to end, turn. 93 [105:117:129] sts.

2nd row: 1 ch (does NOT count as st), 1 dc into each dc to end, turn.

3rd to 5th rows: As 2nd row.

6th row: 1 ch (does NOT count as st), 1 dc into each of first 4 [6:7:9] dc, *1 htr into next dc, 1 dc into each of next 6 dc, 2 htr into next dc, 1 dc into each of next 6 dc, 1 htr into next dc*, 1 dc into each of next 8 [10:14:16] dc, rep from * to * once more, 1 dc into each of next 9 [13:15:19] dc, rep from * to * once more, 1 dc into each of next 8 [10:14:16] dc, rep from * to * once more, 1 dc into each of last 4 [6:7:9] dc, turn. 97 [109:121:133] sts.
Change to 3.5 mm hook.
Now work in patt as follows:

1st row (RS): 1 ch (does NOT count as st), 1 dc into each of first 4 [6:7:9] dc, work first row of patt panel over next 16 sts, 1 dc into each of next 8 [10:14:16] dc, work first row of patt panel over next 16 sts, 1 dc into each of next 9 [13:15:19] dc, work first row of patt panel over next 16 sts, 1 dc into each of next 8 [10:14:16] dc, work first row of patt panel over next 16 sts, 1 dc into each of last 4 [6:7:9] dc, turn.

2nd row: 1 ch (does NOT count as st), 1 dc into each of first 4 [6:7:9] dc, work 2nd row of patt panel over next 16 sts, 1 dc into each of next 8 [10:14:16] dc, work 2nd row of patt panel over next 16 sts, 1 dc into each of next 9 [13:15:19] dc, work 2nd row of patt panel over next 16 sts, 1 dc into each of next 8 [10:14:16] dc, work 2nd row of patt panel over next 16 sts, 1 dc into each of last 4 [6:7:9] dc, turn.
These 2 rows set the sts – 4 patt panels with dc fabric between and at sides.
Cont as set until Body measures 10 [13:16:19] cm, 4 [5:6¼:7½] in.

DIVIDE FOR ARMHOLES

Next row: 1 ch (does NOT count as st), patt 24 [27:30:33] sts and turn, leaving rem sts unworked.
Work on this set of sts only for first front.
Cont straight until work measures 8 [9:9:10] cm, 3 [3½:3½:4] in, from dividing row, ending at armhole edge.

SHAPE NECK

Next row: 1 ch (does NOT count as st), patt to last 4 [5:5:6] sts and turn, leaving rem sts unworked. 20 [22:25:27] sts.

Dec 1 st (by working dc2tog) at neck edge of next 4 rows, then on foll 1 [1:2:2] alt rows. 15 [17:19:21] sts.
Cont straight until work measures 12 [13:14:15] cm, 4¾ [5:5½:6] in, from dividing row.

SHAPE SHOULDER

Fasten off.

SHAPE BACK

Return to last complete row worked, attach yarn to next dc and cont as follows:

Next row: 1 ch (does NOT count as st), patt 49 [55:61:67] sts and turn, leaving rem sts unworked.
Work on this set of 49 [55:61:67] sts only for back.
Cont straight until back matches first front to shoulder.

SHAPE SHOULDER

Fasten off, placing markers at each side of centre 19 [21:23:25] sts to denote back neck.

SHAPE SECOND FRONT

Return to last complete row worked, attach yarn to next dc and cont as follows:

Next row: 1 ch (does NOT count as st), patt to end, turn. 24 [27:30:33] sts.
Complete to match first front, reversing shapings.

Sleeves MAKE 2

With 3 mm hook, make 27 [29:31:33] ch and join with a ss to form a ring.

1st round (RS): 1 ch (does NOT count as st), 1 dc into each ch to end, ss to first dc, turn.

27 [29:31:33] sts.

2nd round: 1 ch (does NOT count as st), 1 dc into each dc to end, ss to first dc, turn.

3rd to 5th rounds: As 2nd round.

6th round: 1 ch (does NOT count as st), 1 dc into each of first 6 [7:8:9] dc, 1 htr into next dc, 1 dc into each of next 6 dc, 2 htr into next dc, 1 dc into each of next 6 dc, 1 htr into next dc, 1 dc into each of last 6 [7:8:9] dc, ss to first dc, turn. 28 [30:32:34] sts. Change to 3.5 mm hook.

Now work in patt as follows:

1st round (RS): 1 ch (does NOT count as st), 2 dc into first dc, 1 dc into each of next 5 [6:7:8] dc, work first row of patt panel over next 16 sts, 1 dc into each of next 5 [6:7:8] dc, 2 dc into last dc, ss to first dc, turn. 30 [32:34:36] sts.

2nd round: 1 ch (does NOT count as st), 2 [1:1:1] dc into first dc, 1 dc into each of next 6 [7:8:9] dc, work 2nd row of patt panel over next 16 sts, 1 dc into each of next 6

[7:8:9] dc, 2 [1:1:1] dc into last dc, ss to first dc, turn. 32 [32:34:36] sts.

These 2 rounds set the sts – central patt panel with dc fabric at sides. Cont as set, inc 1 st (by working twice into first and last dc) at each end of next [next:next:2nd] and 8 [9:6:10] foll alt [alt:alt:3rd] rounds, then at each end of 0 [1:5:2] foll 0 [3rd:3rd:4th] rounds.

50 [54:58:62] sts.

Cont straight until Sleeve measures 13 [16:20:26] cm, 5 [6¼:7¾:10¼] in.

Fasten off.

Making up

Join shoulder seams. Insert sleeves into armholes, matching centre of last row to shoulder seam and top of "sleeve seam" to underarm.

LEFT FRONT EDGING

With RS facing and using 3.00 mm hook, rejoin yarn at start of left front neck shaping, 1 ch (does NOT count as st), work 1 row of dc evenly down entire left front opening edge. Fasten off.

RIGHT FRONT EDGING

With RS facing and using 3 mm hook, rejoin yarn at base of right front opening edge, 1 ch (does NOT count as st), work 1 row of dc evenly up entire right front opening edge to neck shaping.
Do NOT fasten off.

COLLAR

With RS facing, using 3 mm hook and yarn on hook from Right Front Edging, work 1 row of dc evenly around entire neck edge, ending at top of Left Front Edging and ensure number of dc worked is an odd number, turn.

Next row: 1 ch (does NOT count as st), 1 dc into first dc, *2 dc into next dc, 1 dc into next dc, rep from * to end, turn.
Next row: 1 ch (does NOT count as st), 1 dc into each dc to end, turn. Rep last row until Collar measures 6 [6:7:7] cm, 2¼ [2¼:2¾:2¾] in. Fasten off.

Insert zip into front opening.

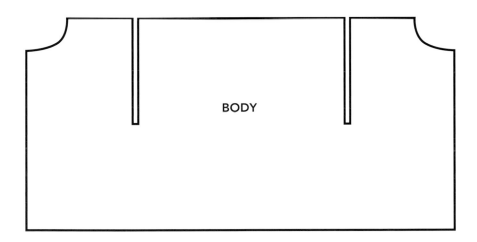

BODY

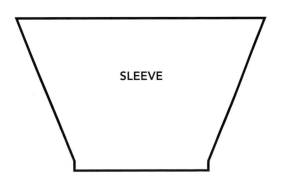

SLEEVE

FRILL-TRIMMED CARDIGAN

Simple stripes of trebles in a classic yarn and double crochet in a fluffy yarn make up this pretty cardigan. Use toning colours to create textured stripes, as here, or choose contrasting colours for a bolder look. The fluffy frill edging finishes off the feminine feel to perfection too!

MEASUREMENTS					
age (months)	0–3	3–6	6–12	12–18	
chest	41	46	51	56	cm
	16	18	20	22	in
actual chest	46	51	56	61	cm
	18	20	22	24	in
full length	23	27	31	34	cm
	9	10½	12	13¼	in
sleeve seam	13	16	19	21	cm
	5	6¼	7½	8¼	in

MATERIALS
- 2 [2:3:3] x 50 g balls of Rowan Cashsoft DK in A (Poppy 512)
- 3 [3:3:3] x 25 g balls of Rowan Kidsilk Haze in B (Cherry red 847). NB: Use 2 strands of this yarn throughout.
- 4 mm crochet hook

ABBREVIATIONS
See page 9.

TENSION
16 stitches and 11½ rows to 10 cm (4 in) measured over pattern using 4 mm hook.
Change hook size if necessary to obtain this tension.

STITCH DIAGRAM

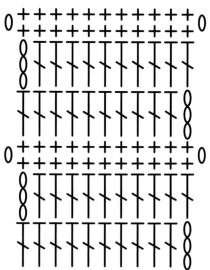

KEY

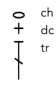

0   ch
+   dc
⊥   tr

Shaping note

Decreases

Work all decreases at beg and ends of rows by working 2 sts together. On first and 4th patt rows, work dec at beg of row by working "3 ch (does NOT count as st – remember NOT to work into top of this 3 ch when working next row), 1 tr into next st – 1 st decreased" and work dec at end of row by working "tr2tog over last 2 sts". On 2nd and 3rd patt rows, work dec at beg of row by working "1 ch (does NOT count as st), dc2tog over first 2 sts – 1 st decreased" and work dec at end of row by working "dc2tog over last 2 sts".
At top of sleeve, dec 2 sts at each end of row by working "1 ss into each of first 3 sts, make turning ch as required, patt to last 2 sts and turn, leaving rem 2 sts unworked".

Increases

Work all increases at beg and ends of rows by working 2 sts into one st of previous row. On first and 4th patt rows, work inc at beg of row by working "3 ch (counts as first tr), 1 tr into st at base of 3 ch – 1 st increased" and work inc at end of row by working "2 tr into last st". On 2nd and 3rd patt rows, work inc at beg of row by working "1 ch (does NOT count as st), 2 dc into first st – 1 st increased" and work inc at end of row by working "2 dc into last st".

Body

(worked in one piece to armholes)
With 4 mm hook and A, make

77 [85:93:101] ch.
Foundation row (RS): 1 tr into 4th ch from hook, 1 tr into each ch to end, turn. 75 [83:91:99] sts.
Now work in patt as follows:
1st row (WS): Using A, 3 ch (counts as first tr), miss tr at base of 3 ch, 1 tr into each tr to end, working last tr into top of 3 ch at beg of previous row, turn.
Join in B.
2nd row: Using B, 1 ch (does NOT count as st), 1 dc into each tr to end, working last dc into top of 3 ch at beg of previous row, turn.
3rd row: Using B, 1 ch (does NOT count as st), 1 dc into each dc to end, turn.
4th row: Using A, 3 ch (counts as first tr), miss dc at base of 3 ch, 1 tr into each dc to end, turn.
These 4 rows form patt.
Cont in patt for another 8 [11:14:17] rows, ending after 1 [2:1:2] rows using A [B:B:A]. (Body should measure approx 11 [14:17:19] cm, 4¼ [5½:6½:7½] in.)

DIVIDE FOR ARMHOLES

Keeping patt and stripes correct, cont as follows:
Next row: Patt 17 [19:21:23] sts and turn, leaving rem sts unworked.
Work on this set of 17 [19:21:23] sts only for first front.
Dec 1 st at each end of next 4 rows. 9 [11:13:15] sts.
Dec 1 st at front slope edge only of next 2 [3:4:5] rows, then on foll 2 alt rows. 5 [6:7:8] sts.
Work 1 row, ending after 1 row using yarn A. (Armhole should measure 10 [11:12:13] cm, 4 [4¼:4¾:5] in.)

SHAPE SHOULDER

Fasten off.

SHAPE BACK

Return to last complete row worked, miss next 4 sts, attach yarn to next st and cont as follows:
Next row: Patt 33 [37:41:45] sts and turn, leaving rem sts unworked.
Work on this set of 33 [37:41:45] sts only for back.
Dec 1 st at each end of next 4 rows. 25 [29:33:37] sts.
Work 7 [8:9:10] rows, ending after 1 row using yarn A.

SHAPE SHOULDER

Fasten off, placing markers at each side of centre 15 [17:19:21] sts to denote back neck.

SHAPE SECOND FRONT

Return to last complete row worked, miss next 4 sts, attach yarn to next st and cont as follows:
Next row: Patt to end, turn.
17 [19:21:23] sts.
Complete to match first front, reversing shapings.

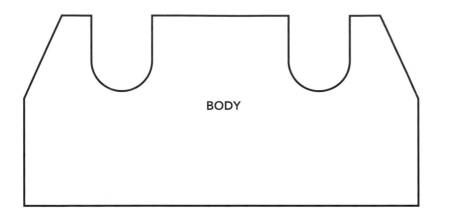

BODY

SLEEVE

Sleeves MAKE 2

With 4 mm hook and A, make 21 [23:25:27] ch.
Work foundation row as given for Body. 19 [21:23:25] sts.
Starting with first patt row, cont in patt as given for Body, inc 1 st at each end of next and foll 5 [6:3:3] alt rows, then on 0 [0:3:4] foll 3rd rows. 31 [35:37:41] sts.
Work 1 [2:2:2] rows, ending after 1 [2:1:2] rows using A [B:B:A]. (Sleeve should measure approx 11 [14:17:19] cm, 4¼ [5½:6½:7½] in.)

SHAPE TOP

Keeping patt and stripes correct, dec 2 sts at each end of next row. 27 [31:33:37] sts.
Dec 1 st at each end of next 6 [7:8:9] rows, ending after 2 rows using B. 15 [17:17:19] sts.
Fasten off.

Making up

Join shoulder seams.

HEM FRILL

With RS facing, using 4 mm hook and B, rejoin yarn at base of left front opening edge, 1 ch (does NOT count as st), work 1 row of dc evenly across entire foundation ch edge of Body, turn.
Next row: 4 ch (counts as first tr and 1 ch), miss dc at base of 4 ch, 1 tr into next dc, *1 ch, 1 tr into next dc, rep from * to end, turn.
Next row: 4 ch (counts as first tr and 1 ch), miss tr at base of 4 ch, *1 tr into next ch sp, 1 ch**, 1 tr into next tr, 1 ch, rep from * to end, ending last rep at **, 1 tr into 3rd of 4 ch at beg of previous row.
Fasten off.

CUFF FRILLS (BOTH ALIKE)

Work as given for Hem frill.

Join sleeve and cuff frill seams. Insert sleeves into armholes, matching centre of last row to shoulder seam and top of sleeve seam to centre of sts missed at underarm.

FRONT AND NECK FRILL

With RS facing, using 4 mm hook and B, rejoin yarn at base of right front opening edge (this is top of last row of Hem frill), 1 ch (does NOT count as st), work 1 row of dc evenly up entire right front opening and neck edge, across back neck, then down entire left from slope and opening edge, turn.
Complete as given for Hem and Cuff frills.

TIES (MAKE 2)

With 4 mm hook and A, make a ch approx 25 cm (9¾ in) long.
Next row: 1 dc into 2nd ch from hook, 1 dc into each ch to end.
Fasten off.

Attach Ties to inside of first row of Front and Neck Frill, level with start of front slope shaping.

COSY CARDIGAN

A classic cardigan for all seasons given a new twist with a versatile textured stitch! The simple two-row pattern uses just basic stitches to create the boxed bobble effect – and it will look just as good on a baby boy or baby girl!

MEASUREMENTS					
age (months)	0–3	3–6	6–12	12–18	
chest	41	46	51	56	cm
	16	18	20	22	in
actual chest	47	54	61	68	cm
	18½	21¼	24	26¾	in
length	23	25	28	34	cm
	9	9¾	11	13¼	in
sleeve seam	13	16	20	25	cm
	5	6¼	7¾	9¾	in

MATERIALS
- 3 [3:4:4] x 50 g balls of Rowan Pure Wool DK in Pier 006
- 3.5 mm and 4 mm crochet hooks
- 5 buttons

ABBREVIATIONS
- **htr3tog** – (yoh and insert hook as indicated, yoh and draw loop through) 3 times, yoh and draw through all 7 loops on hook. See also page 9.

TENSION
17 stitches and 11 rows to 10 cm (4 in) measured over pattern using 4 mm hook.
Change hook size if necessary to obtain this tension.

SHAPING NOTE
When working shaping through patt, work part patt reps as htr fabric (by working 1 htr into each st).

KEY

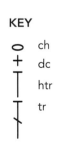

○	ch
+	dc
T	htr
T (tr symbol)	tr

STITCH DIAGRAM

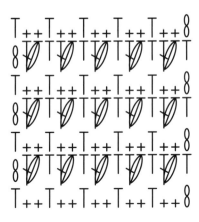

Body

(worked in one piece to armholes)
With 3.5 mm hook, make 77
[89:101:113] ch.
1st row (WS): 1 dc into 2nd ch from
hook, 1 dc into each ch to end, turn.
76 [88:100:112] sts.
2nd row: 1 ch (does NOT count as
st), 1 dc into each dc to end, turn.
3rd to 5th rows: As 2nd row.
Change to 4 mm hook.
6th row: 2 ch (counts as first htr),
miss dc at base of 2 ch, *1 dc into
each of next 2 dc, 1 htr into next dc,
rep from * to end, turn.

Now work in patt as follows:
1st row (WS): 2 ch (counts as first
htr), miss htr at base of 2 ch, *1 tr
into next dc, htr3tog around stem of
tr just worked, miss 1 dc, 1 htr into
next htr, rep from * to end, working
htr at end of last rep into top of
2 ch at beg of previous row, turn.
25 [29:33:37] patt reps.
2nd row: 2 ch (counts as first htr),
miss htr at base of 2 ch, *1 dc into
next htr3tog, 1 dc into next tr,
1 htr into next htr, rep from * to end,
working htr at end of last rep into
top of 2 ch at beg of previous row,
turn.
These 2 rows form patt.
Cont in patt until Body measures
approx 12 [14:15:21] cm (4¾
[5½:6:8¼] in), ending with RS facing
for next row.

DIVIDE FOR ARMHOLES
Next row: 2 ch (counts as first htr),
miss htr at base of 2 ch, [1 dc into
next htr3tog, 1 dc into next tr, 1 htr
into next htr] 5 [6:7:8] times and turn,

leaving rem sts unworked.
Work on this set of 16 [19:22:25] sts
only for right front.
Work 7 rows, ending with RS facing
for next row.

SHAPE NECK
Next row: Ss across and into
5th [8th:6th:6th] st – 4 [7:5:5] sts
decreased, 2 ch (counts as first htr),
miss st at base of 2 ch, patt to end,
turn. 12 [12:17:20] sts.
Next row: Patt 11 [11:16:19] sts and
turn, leaving rem st unworked – 1 st
decreased.
Next row: Ss across and into 2nd st
– 1 st decreased, 2 ch (counts as first
htr), miss st at base of 2 ch, patt to
end, turn. 10 [10:15:18] sts.

3rd and 4th sizes only
Next row: Patt [14:17] sts and turn,
leaving rem sts unworked – 1 st
decreased.
Next row: Ss across and into 2nd st
– 1 st decreased, 2 ch (counts as first
htr), miss st at base of 2 ch, patt to
end, turn. [13:16] sts.

All sizes
Work 2 rows, ending with WS facing
for next row.

SHAPE SHOULDER
Fasten off.

SHAPE BACK
Return to last complete row worked,
miss next 5 sts, attach yarn to next st
and cont as follows:
Next row: 2 ch (counts as first htr),
miss st at base of 2 ch, patt 33
[39:45:51] sts and turn, leaving rem
sts unworked.
Work on this set of 34 [40:46:52] sts

only for back.
Work 12 [12:14:14] rows, ending with
WS facing for next row.

SHAPE SHOULDER
Fasten off, placing markers at each
side of centre 14 [20:20:20] sts to
denote back neck.

SHAPE LEFT FRONT
Return to last complete row worked,
miss next 5 sts, attach yarn to next st
and cont as follows:
Next row: 2 ch (counts as first htr),
miss st at base of 2 ch, patt to end,
turn. 16 [19:22:25] sts.
Complete to match right front,
reversing shapings.

Sleeves

With 3.5 mm hook, make 23
[26:26:29] ch.
1st row (WS): 1 dc into 2nd ch from
hook, 1 dc into each ch to end, turn.
22 [25:25:28] sts.
2nd row: 1 ch (does NOT count as
st), 1 dc into each dc to end, turn.
3rd to 5th rows: As 2nd row.
Change to 4 mm hook.
6th row: 2 ch (counts as first htr),
miss dc at base of 2 ch, *1 dc into
each of next 2 dc, 1 htr into next dc,
rep from * to end, turn.
Now work in patt as follows:
1st row (WS): 2 ch (counts as first
htr), 1 htr into htr at base of
2 ch – 1 st increased, *1 tr into next
dc, htr3tog around stem of tr just
worked, miss 1 dc**, 1 htr into next
htr, rep from * to end, ending last
rep at **, 2 htr into top of 2 ch at
beg of previous row – 1 st increased,
turn. 24 [27:27:30] sts.

Working all increases as set by last row and working inc sts in htr fabric until there are sufficient to work in patt, cont as follows:
Work 0 [1:1:2] rows.
Inc 1 st at each end of next 4 [1:1:1] rows, then on foll 2 [3:7:0] alt rows, then on 0 [1:0:6] foll 3rd rows. 36 [37:43:44] sts.
Work 1 [2:1:2] rows, ending with WS facing for next row.

SHAPE TOP
Place markers at both ends of last row to denote top of sleeve seam.
Work another 2 rows.
Fasten off.

Making up

Join shoulder seams. Join sleeve seams. Insert sleeves into armholes, matching centre of last row to shoulder seam and top of sleeve seam to centre of sts missed at underarm.

NECKBAND
With RS facing and using 3.5 mm hook, rejoin yarn at top of right front opening edge, 1 ch (does NOT count as st), work 1 row of dc evenly around entire neck edge, ending at top of left front opening edge, turn.
Next row: 1 ch (does NOT count as st), 1 dc into each dc to end, working dc2tog as required to ensure Neckband lies flat, turn.
Rep last row 3 times more.
Fasten off.

BUTTON BAND
With RS facing and using 3.5 mm hook, rejoin yarn at top of left end of Neckband for a girl, or base of right front opening edge for a boy, 1 ch (does NOT count as st), work 1 row of dc evenly along entire front opening edge, between top of Neckband and foundation ch edge.
1st row: 1 ch (does NOT count as st), 1 dc into each dc to end, turn.
Rep last row 3 times more.
Fasten off.

Mark positions for 5 buttons on this Band – first to come 12 mm (½ in) up from lower edge, last to come 12 mm (½ in) down from top of Neckband, and rem 3 buttons evenly spaced between.

BUTTONHOLE BAND
Work to match Button Band, making buttonholes in 3rd row to correspond with positions marked for buttons by replacing "1 dc into each of next 2 dc" with "2 ch, miss 2 dc". (On foll row, work 2 dc into this buttonhole ch sp.)

Sew on buttons.

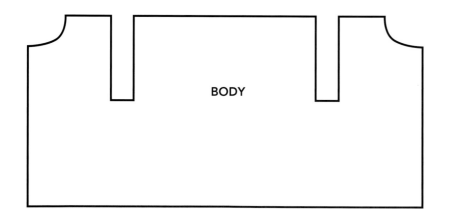

BODY

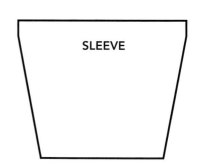

SLEEVE

DUFFLE COAT

Made in a really chunky pure wool yarn, using just double crochet, you will have this cosy coat made in no time. And its clever construction means there are virtually no seams to sew up afterwards – making it even easier to complete!

MEASUREMENTS					
age (months)	0–3	3–6	6–12	12–18	
chest	41	46	51	56	cm
	16	18	20	22	in
actual chest	46	54	60	67	cm
	18	21¼	23½	26¼	in
length	28	34	40	44	cm
	11	13¼	15¾	17¼	in
sleeve seam	12	15	20	23	cm
	4¾	6	7¾	9	in

MATERIALS
• 4 [5:5:6] x 100 g balls of Rowan Big Wool in Glamour 036
• 7 mm crochet hook
• 3 buttons

ABBREVIATIONS
See page 9.

TENSION
9 stitches and 10 rows to 10 cm (4 in) measured over pattern using 7 mm hook.
Change hook size if necessary to obtain this tension.

STITCH DIAGRAM

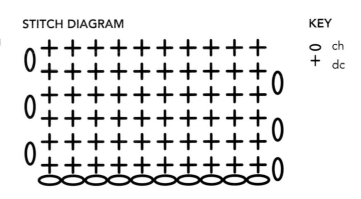

KEY
o ch
+ dc

Body

(worked in one piece to armholes)
With 7 mm hook, make 61 [72:81:92] ch.

1st row (RS): 1 dc into 2nd ch from hook, 1 dc into each ch to end, turn. 60 [71:80:91] sts.

2nd row: 1 ch (does NOT count as st), 1 dc into each st to end, turn. This row forms patt.
Work 2 rows.

5th row: 1 ch (does NOT count as st), 1 dc into each of first 8 [9:9:10] dc, dc2tog over next 2 dc, (1 dc into each of next 12 [15:18:21] dc, dc2tog over next 2 dc) 3 times, 1 dc into each of last 8 [9:9:10] dc, turn. 56 [67:76:87] sts.
Work 3 rows.

9th row: 1 ch (does NOT count as st), 1 dc into each of first 6 [7:7:11] dc, dc2tog over next 2 dc, (1 dc into each of next 12 [15:18:19] dc, dc2tog over next 2 dc) 3 times, 1 dc into each of last 6 [7:7:11] dc, turn. 52 [63:72:83] sts. Work 3 rows.

13th row: 1 ch (does NOT count as st), 1 dc into each of first 7 [8:8:9] dc, dc2tog over next 2 dc, (1 dc into each of next 10 [13:16:19] dc, dc2tog over next 2 dc) 3 times, 1 dc into each of last 7 [8:8:9] dc, turn. 48 [59:68:79] sts.

2nd, 3rd and 4th sizes only

Work 3 rows.

17th row: 1 ch (does NOT count as st), 1 dc into each of first [6:6:10] dc, dc2tog over next 2 dc, (1 dc into each of next [13:16:17] dc, dc2tog over next 2 dc) 3 times, 1 dc into each of last [6:6:10] dc, turn. [55:64:75] sts.

3rd and 4th sizes only

Work 3 rows.

21st row: 1 ch (does NOT count as st), 1 dc into each of first [7:8] dc, dc2tog over next 2 dc, (1 dc into each of next [14:17] dc, dc2tog over next 2 dc) 3 times, 1 dc into each of last [7:8] dc, turn. [60:71] sts.

4th size only

Work 3 rows.

25th row: 1 ch (does NOT count as st), 1 dc into each of first 9 dc, dc2tog over next 2 dc, (1 dc into each of next 15 dc, dc2tog over next 2 dc) 3 times, 1 dc into each of last 9 dc, turn. 67 sts.

All sizes

Work 3 [4:5:4] rows on rem 48 [55:60:67] sts, ending with RS [WS:RS:WS] facing for next row. Break yarn.

Sleeves

With 7 mm hook, make 12 [13:14:15] ch and join with a ss to form a ring.

1st round (RS): 1 ch (does NOT count as st), 1 dc into each ch to end, ss to first dc, turn. 12 [13:14:15] sts.

Note: You must turn at the end of every round so that the sleeve fabric matches the body fabric.

2nd round: 1 ch (does NOT count as st), 1 dc into each dc to end, ss to first dc, turn.
This round forms patt.

3rd round: 1 ch (does NOT count as st), 2 dc into first dc – 1 st increased, 1 dc into each dc to last dc, 2 dc into last dc – 1 st increased, ss to first dc, turn. 14 [15:16:17] sts.
Working all increases as set by last round, inc 1 st at each end of 2nd [2nd:3rd:3rd] and foll 3 [1:0:0] alt rounds, then on 0 [2:4:2] foll 3rd rounds, then on 0 [0:0:2] foll 4th rounds. 22 [23:26:27] sts.
Work 1 [2:2:3] rounds, ending with RS [WS:RS:WS] facing for next round. Break yarn.

Yoke

With RS [WS:RS:WS] facing and 7 mm hook, rejoin yarn to last st of last row of Body and join Body and Sleeves as follows:

1st row: 1 ch (does NOT count as st), 1 dc into each of first 11 [13:14:16] dc of Body, miss first 2 dc of next round of first Sleeve, 1 dc into each of next 18 [19:22:23] dc of Sleeve, miss last 2 dc of Sleeve and next 4 dc of Body, 1 dc into each of next 18 [21:24:27] dc of Body, miss first 2 dc of next round of second Sleeve, 1 dc into each of next 18 [19:22:23] dc of Sleeve, miss last 2 dc of Sleeve and next 4 dc of Body, 1 dc into each of last 11 [13:14:16] dc of Body, turn. 76 [85:96:105] sts.

2nd row: 1 ch (does NOT count as st), 1 dc into each of first 11 [13:14:14] dc, *(dc2tog over next 2 dc) 1 [1:1:2] times, 1 dc into each of next 14 [15:18:19] dc, (dc2tog over next 2 dc) 1 [1:1:2] times*, 1 dc into each of next 18 [21:24:23] dc, rep from * to * once more, 1 dc into each of last 11 [13:14:14] dc, turn. 72 [81:92:97] sts.

3rd row: 1 ch (does NOT count as st), 1 dc into each of first 11 [13:12:15] dc, *(dc2tog over next 2 dc) 1 [1:2:1] times, 1 dc into each of next 12 [13:16:17] dc, (dc2tog

over next 2 dc) 1 [1:2:1] times*, 1 dc into each of next 18 [21:20:25] dc, rep from * to * once more, 1 dc into each of last 11 [13:12:15] dc, turn. 68 [77:84:93] sts.

4th row: 1 ch (does NOT count as st), 1 dc into each of first 9 [11:13:13] dc, *(dc2tog over next 2 dc) 2 [2:1:2] times, 1 dc into each of next 10 [11:14:15] dc, (dc2tog over next 2 dc) 2 [2:1:2] times*, 1 dc into each of next 14 [17:22:21] dc, rep from * to * once more, 1 dc into each of last 9 [11:13:13] dc, turn. 60 [69:80:85] sts.

5th row: 1 ch (does NOT count as st), 1 dc into each of first 10 [12:11:14] dc, *(dc2tog over next 2 dc) 1 [1:2:1] times, 1 dc into each of next 8 [9:12:13] dc, (dc2tog over next 2 dc) 1 [1:2:1] times*, 1 dc into each of next 16 [19:18:23] dc, rep from * to * once more, 1 dc into each of last 10 [12:11:14] dc, turn. 56 [65:72:81] sts.

6th row: 1 ch (does NOT count as st), 1 dc into each of first 10 [10:12:12] dc, *(dc2tog over next 2 dc) 1 [2:1:2] times, 1 dc into each of next 6 [7:10:11] dc, (dc2tog over next 2 dc) 1 [2:1:2] times*, 1 dc into each of next 16 [15:20:19] dc, rep from * to * once more, 1 dc into each of last 10 [10:12:12] dc, turn. 52 [57:68:73] sts.

7th row: 1 ch (does NOT count as st), 1 dc into each of first 8 [11:10:13] dc, *(dc2tog over next 2 dc) 2 [0:2:0] times, 1 dc into each of next 4 [9:8:13] dc, (dc2tog over next 2 dc) 2 [0:2:0] times*, 1 dc into each of next 12 [17:16:21] dc, rep from * to * once more, 1 dc into each of last 8 [11:10:13] dc, turn. 44 [57:60:73] sts.

8th row: 1 ch (does NOT count as st), 1 dc into each of first 9 [9:11:11] dc, *(dc2tog over next 2 dc) 0 [2:0:2] times, 1 dc into each of next 6 [5:10:9] dc, (dc2tog over next 2 dc) 0 [2:0:2] times*, 1 dc into each of next 14 [13:18:17] dc, rep from * to * once more, 1 dc into each of last 9 [9:11:11] dc, turn. 44 [49:60:65] sts.

9th row: 1 ch (does NOT count as st), 1 dc into each of first 7 [10:9:12] dc, *(dc2tog over next 2 dc) 2 [0:2:0] times, 1 dc into each of next 2 [7:6:11] dc, (dc2tog over next 2 dc) 2 [0:2:0] times*, 1 dc into each of next 10 [15:14:19] dc, rep from * to * once more, 1 dc into each of last 7 [10:9:12] dc, turn. 36 [49:52:65] sts.

10th row: 1 ch (does NOT count as st), 1 dc into each of first 8 [8:10:10] dc, *(dc2tog over next 2 dc) 0 [2:0:2] times, 1 dc into each of next 4 [3:8:7] dc, (dc2tog over next 2 dc) 0 [2:0:2] times*, 1 dc into each of next 12 [11:16:15] dc, rep from * to * once more, 1 dc into each of last 8 [8:10:10] dc, turn. 36 [41:52:57] sts.

11th row: 1 ch (does NOT count as st), 1 dc into each of first 6 [9:8:11] dc, *(dc2tog over next 2 dc) 2 [0:2:0] times, 1 dc into each of next 0 [5:4:9] dc, (dc2tog over next 2 dc) 2 [0:2:0] times*, 1 dc into each of next 8 [13:12:17] dc, rep from * to * once more, 1 dc into each of last 6 [9:8:11] dc, turn. 28 [41:44:57] sts.

2nd, 3rd and 4th sizes only

12th row: 1 ch (does NOT count as st), 1 dc into each of first [7:9:9] dc, *(dc2tog over next 2 dc) [2:0:2] times, 1 dc into each of next [1:6:5] dc, (dc2tog over next 2 dc) [2:0:2] times*, 1 dc into each of next [9:14:13] dc, rep from * to * once

more, 1 dc into each of last [7:9:9] dc, turn. [33:44:49] sts.

3rd and 4th sizes only

13th row: 1 ch (does NOT count as st), 1 dc into each of first [7:10] dc, *(dc2tog over next 2 dc) [2:0] times, 1 dc into each of next [2:7] dc, (dc2tog over next 2 dc) [2:0] times*, 1 dc into each of next [10:15] dc, rep from * to * once more, 1 dc into each of last [7:10] dc, turn. [36:49] sts.

4th size only

14th row: 1 ch (does NOT count as st), 1 dc into each of first 8 dc, *(dc2tog over next 2 dc) twice, 1 dc into each of next 3 dc, (dc2tog over next 2 dc) twice*, 1 dc into each of next 11 dc, rep from * to * once more, 1 dc into each of last 8 dc, turn. 41 sts.

All sizes

Next row (WS): 1 ch (does NOT count as st), 1 dc into each dc to end, turn. 28 [33:36:41] sts.

SHAPE FOR HOOD

Next row: 1 ch (does NOT count as st), 1 dc into each of first 3 [2:3:2] dc, (dc2tog over next 2 dc, 1 dc into each of next 2 dc) 5 [3:7:4] times, (dc2tog over next 2 dc, 1 dc into next dc) 0 [1:0:1] times, (dc2tog over next 2 dc, 1 dc into each of next 2 dc) 0 [3:0:4] times, dc2tog over next 2 dc, 1 dc into each of last 3 [2:3:2] dc, turn. 22 [25:28:31] sts. Work 1 row.

Next row: 1 ch (does NOT count as st), 1 dc into each of first 7 [9:11:13] dc, 2 dc into each of next 8 [7:6:5] dc, 1 dc into each of last 7 [9:11:13] dc, turn. 30 [32:34:36] sts.

Work 14 [15:16:17] rows.

Next row: 1 ch (does NOT count as st), 1 dc into each of first 13 [14:15:16] dc, (dc2tog over next 2 dc) twice, 1 dc into each of last 13 [14:15:16] dc, turn. 28 [30:32:34] sts.

Work 1 row.

Next row: 1 ch (does NOT count as st), 1 dc into each of first 12 [13:14:15] dc, (dc2tog over next 2 dc) twice, 1 dc into each of last 12 [13:14:15] dc, turn. 26 [28:30:32] sts.

Next row: 1 ch (does NOT count as st), 1 dc into each of first 11 [12:13:14] dc, (dc2tog over next 2 dc) twice, 1 dc into each of last 11 [12:13:14] dc, turn. 24 [26:28:30] sts.

Fold Hood in half with RS together and join top of Hood by working 1 row of dc through both layers. Fasten off.

Making up

Join underarm seams. Sew on buttons, placing buttons on 3rd st in from front opening edge (on left front for a girl, or right front for a boy), positioning lowest button 8 [10:12:14] cm (3 [4:4¾:5½] in) up from lower edge, top button 6 [6:7:7] cm (2¼ [2¼:2¾:2¾] in) down from first row of Hood and rem button evenly spaced between. Push buttons through fabric of other front to fasten.

PRAM BLANKET

The fully reversible stitch used for this cosy blanket means it will look just as good whichever way baby snuggles up. And the soft, machine washable cotton and microfibre yarn makes it practical too. Choose a strong shade, as here, or a pretty pastel colour – either way it is bound to keep baby cosy.

MEASUREMENTS		
Finished size	70 x 90	cm
	27½ x 35½	in

MATERIALS
- 14 x 50 g balls of Rowan All Seasons Cotton in Dark violet 257
- 5 mm crochet hook

ABBREVIATIONS
- **htr3tog** – (yoh and insert hook as indicated, yoh and draw loop through) 3 times, yoh and draw through all 7 loops on hook.
See also page 9

TENSION
15 stitches and 9 rows to 10 cm (4 in) measured over pattern using 5 mm hook.
Change hook size if necessary to obtain this tension.

STITCH DIAGRAM

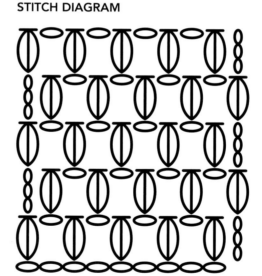

KEY
- ⬭ ch
- ⬭ htr3tog

Blanket

With 5 mm hook, make 102 ch.
1st row (RS): 1 htr3tog into 4th ch from hook, *1 ch, miss 1 ch, 1 htr3tog into next ch, rep from * to end, turn. 100 sts.
2nd row: 3 ch (counts as first st), miss htr3tog at base of 3 ch, 1 htr3tog into next ch sp, *1 ch, miss 1 htr3tog, 1 htr3tog into next ch sp, rep from * to end, working last htr3tog between htr3tog and 3 ch at beg of previous row, turn.
This row forms patt.
Cont in patt until Blanket measures 87 cm (34¼ in).
Fasten off.

Making up

BORDER

With RS facing and using 5 mm hook, rejoin yarn to outer edge of Blanket, 1 ch (does NOT count as st), work 1 round of dc evenly around entire outer edge, working 3 dc into each corner point and ending with ss to first dc, turn.
Next round: 1 ch (does NOT count as st), 1 dc into each dc to end, working 3 dc into each corner point and ending with ss to first dc.
Fasten off.

HAT, BOOTEES AND MITTS

This classic winter set is given a modern look by being made in a clever multicoloured and hand-dyed yarn. Worked in rounds of simple double crochet, the set is really easy to make and there are almost no seams to sew up when you finish.

MEASUREMENTS					
age (months)	0–3	3–6	6–12	12–18	
HAT					
width around head	34	37	40	43	cm
	13¼	14½	15¾	17	in
BOOTEES					
length of foot	10	11	12	13	cm
	4	4¼	4¾	5	in
MITTS					
width around hand	9	10	11	12	cm
	3½	4	4¼	4¼	in

MATERIALS
- 1 [2:2:2] x 110 g hanks of Colinette Jitterbug in Mardi Gras 155
- 2.5 mm crochet hook

ABBREVIATIONS
See page 9.

TENSION
21 stitches and 26 rows to 10 cm (4 in) measured over dc fabric using 2.5 mm hook. Change hook size if necessary to obtain this tension.

STITCH DIAGRAM

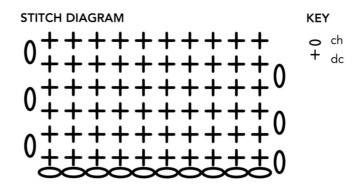

KEY
o ch
+ dc

Hat

With 2.5 mm hook, make 72 [78:84:90] ch and join with a ss to form a ring.

1st round (RS): 1 ch (does NOT count as st), 1 dc into each ch to end, ss to first dc, turn. 72 [78:84:90] sts.

2nd round: 1 ch (does NOT count as st), 1 dc into each dc to end, ss to first dc, turn.

This round forms dc fabric.

Cont in dc fabric until Hat measures 13 cm (5 in), ending with RS facing for next round.

4th size only

Next round (RS): 1 ch (does NOT count as st), (1 dc into each of next 13 dc, dc2tog over next 2 dc) 6 times, ss to first dc, turn. 84 sts.

Work 1 round, ending with RS facing for next round.

3rd and 4th sizes only

Next round (RS): 1 ch (does NOT count as st), (1 dc into each of next 12 dc, dc2tog over next 2 dc) 6 times, ss to first dc, turn. 78 sts.

Work 1 round, ending with RS facing for next round.

2nd, 3rd and 4th sizes only

Next round (RS): 1 ch (does NOT count as st), (1 dc into each of next 11 dc, dc2tog over next 2 dc) 6 times, ss to first dc, turn. 72 sts.

Work 1 round, ending with RS facing for next round.

All sizes

Next round (RS): 1 ch (does NOT count as st), (1 dc into each of next 10 dc, dc2tog over next 2 dc) 6

times, ss to first dc, turn. 66 sts.

Work 1 round.

Next round: 1 ch (does NOT count as st), (1 dc into each of next 9 dc, dc2tog over next 2 dc) 6 times, ss to first dc, turn. 60 sts.

Next round: 1 ch (does NOT count as st), (dc2tog over next 2 dc, 1 dc into each of next 8 dc) 6 times, ss to first dc, turn. 54 sts.

Next round: 1 ch (does NOT count as st), (1 dc into each of next 7 dc, dc2tog over next 2 dc) 6 times, ss to first dc, turn. 48 sts.

Next round: 1 ch (does NOT count as st), (dc2tog over next 2 dc, 1 dc into each of next 6 dc) 6 times, ss to first dc, turn. 42 sts.

Next round: 1 ch (does NOT count as st), (1 dc into each of next 5 dc, dc2tog over next 2 dc) 6 times, ss to first dc, turn. 36 sts.

Next round: 1 ch (does NOT count as st), (dc2tog over next 2 dc, 1 dc into each of next 4 dc) 6 times, ss to first dc, turn. 30 sts.

Next round: 1 ch (does NOT count as st), (1 dc into each of next 3 dc, dc2tog over next 2 dc) 6 times, ss to first dc, turn. 24 sts.

Next round: 1 ch (does NOT count as st), (dc2tog over next 2 dc, 1 dc into each of next 2 dc) 6 times, ss to first dc, turn. 18 sts.

Next round: 1 ch (does NOT count as st), (1 dc into next dc, dc2tog over next 2 dc) 6 times, ss to first dc, turn. 12 sts.

Next round: 1 ch (does NOT count as st), (dc2tog over next 2 dc) 6 times, ss to first dc, turn. 6 sts.

Work 6 rounds.

Fasten off.

MAKING UP

Run a gathering thread around top of last round of Hat, pull up tight and fasten off securely. Fold turn-back to RS around lower edge of Hat.

Bootees MAKE 2 ALIKE

With 2.5 mm hook, make 24 [27:30:33] ch and join with a ss to form a ring.

1st round (RS): 1 ch (does NOT count as st), 1 dc into each ch to end, ss to first dc, turn. 24 [27:30:33] sts.

2nd round: 1 ch (does NOT count as st), 1 dc into each dc to end, ss to first dc, turn.

This round forms dc fabric.

Cont in dc fabric until Bootee measures 7 cm (2¾ in), ending with RS facing for next round.

SHAPE INSTEP

Miss first 9 [10:11:12] dc of next round, join in new ball of yarn to next dc, 1 ch (does NOT count as st), 1 dc into dc where yarn was rejoined, 1 dc into each of next 5 [6:7:8] dc, turn.

Next row: 1 ch (does NOT count as st), 1 dc into each dc to end, turn. 6 [7:8:9] sts.

Rep last row 8 [8:10:10] times more. Break yarn.

SHAPE FOOT

Return to last complete round worked and cont as follows:

1 ch (does NOT count as st), 1 dc into each of first 9 [10:11:12] dc, 9 [10:11:12] dc evenly up row-end edge of instep, 1 dc into each of 6 [7:8:9] instep sts, 9 [10:11:12] dc evenly down other row-end edge of

instep, 1 dc into each of last
9 [10:11:12] dc, ss to first dc, turn.
42 [47:52:57] sts.
Work 5 rounds, ending with RS
facing for next round.

SHAPE SOLE
Next round: 1 ch (does NOT count
as st), *1 dc into each of next
3 [3:4:4] dc, dc2tog over next 2 dc,
1 dc into each of next 11 [13:14:16]
dc, dc2tog over next 2 dc, 1 dc into
each of next 3 [3:4:4] dc*, (1 dc into
next dc) 0 [1:0:1] times, rep from * to
* once more, ss to first dc, turn.
38 [43:48:53] sts.
Work 1 round.
Next round: 1 ch (does NOT count
as st), *1 dc into each of next
2 [2:3:3] dc, dc2tog over next 2 dc,
1 dc into each of next 11 [13:14:16]
dc, dc2tog over next 2 dc, 1 dc into
each of next 2 [2:3:3] dc*, (1 dc into
next dc) 0 [1:0:1] times, rep from * to
* once more, ss to first dc, turn.
34 [39:44:49] sts.
Next round: 1 ch (does NOT count
as st), *1 dc into each of next
1 [1:2:2] dc, dc2tog over next 2 dc,

1 dc into each of next 11 [13:14:16]
dc, dc2tog over next 2 dc, 1 dc into
each of next 1 [1:2:2] dc*, (1 dc into
next dc) 0 [1:0:1] times, rep from * to
* once more, ss to first dc, turn.
30 [35:40:45] sts.
Next round: 1 ch (does NOT count
as st), * 1 dc into each of next 0
[0:1:1] dc, dc2tog over next 2 dc,
1 dc into each of next 11 [13:14:16]
dc, dc2tog over next 2 dc, 1 dc into
each of next 0 [0:1:1] dc^, (1 dc into
next dc) 0 [1:0:1] times, rep from * to
* once more, ss to first dc, turn.
26 [31:36:41] sts.
Fasten off.

MAKING UP
Join sole seam. Fold turn-back to RS
around top of Bootee.

Mitts MAKE 2 ALIKE

With 2.5 mm hook, make 20
[22:24:26] ch and join with a ss to
form a ring.
1st round (RS): 1 ch (does NOT count
as st), 1 dc into each ch to end, ss to

first dc, turn. 20 [22:24:26] sts.
2nd round: 1 ch (does NOT count
as st), 1 dc into each dc to end, ss to
first dc, turn.
This round forms dc fabric.
Cont in dc fabric until Mitt measures
6.5 [7:7.5:8] cm (2½ [2¾:3:3¼] in).

SHAPE TOP
Next round: 1 ch (does NOT count
as st), (dc2tog over next 2 dc, 1 dc
into each of next 6 [7:8:9] dc, dc2tog
over next 2 dc) twice, ss to first dc,
turn. 16 [18:20:22] sts.
Work 1 round.
Next round: 1 ch (does NOT count
as st), (dc2tog over next 2 dc, 1 dc
into each of next 4 [5:6:7] dc, dc2tog
over next 2 dc) twice, ss to first dc,
turn. 12 [14:16:18] sts.
Next round: 1 ch (does NOT count
as st), (dc2tog over next 2 dc, 1 dc
into each of next 2 [3:4:5] dc, dc2tog
over next 2 dc) twice, ss to first dc,
turn. 8 [10:12:14] sts.
Fasten off.

MAKING UP
Join top seam.

LACY CARDIGAN

Keep your little angel pretty in pink with this soft and fluffy cardigan. The simple lacy stitch, made up of a combination of trebles and chains, and the minimum of shaping makes it quick and easy to make too. The addition of a classic picot edging completes the look.

MEASUREMENTS					
age (months)	0–3	3–6	6–12	12–18	
chest	41	46	51	56	cm
	16	18	20	22	in
actual chest	50	55	60	65	cm
	19½	21½	23½	25½	in
length	21	25	30	34	cm
	8¼	9¾	11¾	13¼	in
sleeve seam	13	17	20	27	cm
	5	6½	7¾	10½	in

MATERIALS
- 3 [3:4:4] x 50 g balls of Rowan Kid Classic in Tea rose 854
- 4 mm and 4.5 mm crochet hooks
- 5 buttons

ABBREVIATIONS
See page 9.

TENSION
4 pattern repeats and 7 rows to 10 cm (4 in) measured over pattern using 4.5 mm hook.
Change hook size if necessary to produce correct tension.

STITCH DIAGRAM

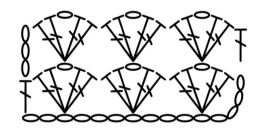

KEY

o   ch

⊤   tr

Body

(worked in one piece to armholes)
With 4.5 mm hook, make 83 [95:99:111] ch loosely.

Foundation row (RS): (2 tr, 1 ch and 2 tr) into 5th ch from hook, *miss 3 ch, (2 tr, 1 ch and 2 tr) into next ch, rep from * to last 2 ch, miss 1 ch, 1 tr into last ch, turn. 102 [117:122:137] sts, 20 [23:24:27] patt reps.

1st row: 3 ch (counts as first tr), miss tr at base of 3 ch and next 2 tr, *(2 tr, 1 ch and 2 tr) into next ch sp**, miss 4 tr, rep from * to end, ending last rep at **, miss 2 tr, 1 tr into top of 3 ch at beg of previous row, turn. This row forms patt.

Work in patt for another 5 [7:9:11] rows, ending with WS facing for next row. Body should measure 10 [13:16:19] cm (4 [5:6¼:7½] in).

DIVIDE FOR ARMHOLES

Next row (WS): Patt first 21 [26:26:31] sts ending after "(2 tr, 1 ch and 2 tr) into next ch sp", miss 2 tr, 1 tr into next tr and turn, leaving rem sts unworked.
Work on this set of 22 [27:27:32] sts, 4 [5:5:6] patt reps only for left front. Work 3 [4:4:5] rows, ending with WS [RS:RS:WS] facing for next row.

SHAPE NECK
1ST AND 4TH SIZES ONLY

Next row: Ss across and into 11th [16th] st, 3 ch (counts as first tr), miss next 2 tr, (2 tr, 1 ch and 2 tr) into next ch sp, patt to end, turn. 12 [17] sts, 2 [3] patt reps.

2ND AND 3RD SIZES ONLY

Next row: Patt first [11:16] sts ending after "(2 tr, 1 ch and 2 tr) into next ch sp", miss 2 tr, 1 tr into next tr and turn, leaving rem sts unworked. [12:17] sts, [2:3] patt reps.

ALL SIZES

Work 2 [2:3:3] rows.

SHAPE SHOULDER

Fasten off.

SHAPE BACK

Return to last complete row worked, miss next 8 sts, attach yarn to next tr and cont as follows:

Next row: 3 ch (counts as first tr), miss tr at base of 3 ch and next 2 tr, *(2 tr, 1 ch and 2 tr) into next ch sp, miss 4 tr, rep from * 6 [7:8:9] times more, (2 tr, 1 ch and 2 tr) into next ch sp, miss 2 tr, 1 tr into next tr and turn, leaving rem sts unworked.
Work on this set of 42 [47:52:57] sts, 8 [9:10:11] patt reps only for back. Work 6 [7:8:9] rows.

SHAPE SHOULDER

Fasten off, placing markers at each side of centre 4 [5:4:5] patt reps to denote back neck.

SHAPE RIGHT FRONT

Return to last complete row worked, miss next 8 sts, attach yarn to next tr and cont as follows:

Next row: 3 ch (counts as first tr), miss tr at base of 3 ch and next 2 tr, (2 tr, 1 ch and 2 tr) into next ch sp,

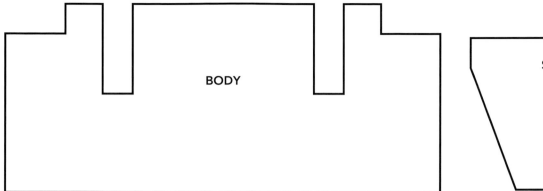

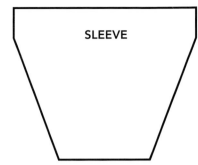

BODY

SLEEVE

patt to end, turn. 22 [27:27:32] sts, 4 [5:5:6] patt reps.
Complete to match left front, reversing shapings.

Sleeves MAKE 2

With 4.5 mm hook, make 23 [23:27:27] ch loosely.
Work foundation row as given for Body. 27 [27:32:32] sts, 5 [5:6:6] patt reps.
1st row: 3 ch (counts as first tr), 1 tr into tr at base of 3 ch — 1 st increased, miss next 2 tr, *(2 tr, 1 ch and 2 tr) into next ch sp**, miss 4 tr, rep from * to end, ending last rep at **, miss 2 tr, 2 tr into top of 3 ch at beg of previous row – 1 st increased, turn.
Working all increases as set by last row, inc 1 st at each end of next 6 [9:7:6] rows, then on foll 0 [0:2:5] alt rows, working inc sts as trs until there are sufficient to work in patt. 41 [47:52:56] sts.
Work 2 rows.
Fasten off.
Place markers along row-end edges 2 cm (¾ in) down from top of last row to denote top of sleeve seam.

Making up

Join shoulder seams. Join sleeve seams. Insert sleeves into armholes, matching centre of last row of sleeve to shoulder seam and top of sleeve seam to centre of sts missed at underarm.

NECK, FRONT AND HEM EDGING

With RS facing and using 4 mm hook, rejoin yarn to foundation ch edge directly below left armhole, 1 ch (does NOT count as st), work 1 round of dc evenly around entire hem, front opening and neck edges, working 3 dc into corners, ensuring number of dc worked is divisible by 4 and ending with ss to first dc, turn.
Mark positions for 5 buttonholes along right front opening edge – first to come 5 cm (2 in) above foundation ch edge, last to come level with start of neck shaping, and rem 3 buttonholes evenly spaced between.
Next round: 1 ch (does NOT count as st), * 1 dc into each of next 2 dc, 3 ch, ss to top of dc just worked, 1 dc into each of next 2 dc, rep from * to end, working 3 dc into corner

points, making buttonholes to correspond with positions marked by replacing "1 dc into next dc" with " 1 ch, miss 1 dc" and ending with ss to first dc.
Fasten off.

CUFF EDGINGS (BOTH ALIKE)

With RS facing and using 4 mm hook, rejoin yarn to foundation ch edge at base of sleeve seam, 1 ch (does NOT count as st), work 1 round of dc evenly around cuff edge, ensuring number of dc worked is divisible by 4 and ending with ss to first dc, turn.
Next round: 1 ch (does NOT count as st), * 1 dc into each of next 2 dc, 3 ch, ss to top of dc just worked, 1 dc into each of next 2 dc, rep from * to end, ss to first dc.
Fasten off.

Sew on buttons.

STRIPED HAT AND SCARF

Keep your little one cosy on the coldest of days with this clever hat and scarf combination. Worked in a soft and fluffy woollen yarn, with bright contrasting stripes, it takes almost no time to make! The multicoloured tassels add the prefect fun finishing touch.

MEASUREMENTS					
age (months)	0–3	3–6	6–12	12–18	
HAT					
width around head	31	34	37	40	cm
	12¼	13¼	14¼	15¾	in
SCARF					
width	10	11	11	12	cm
	4	4¼	4¼	4¾	in
length, excluding tassels	80	90	100	110	cm
	31¼	35¼	39¼	43¼	in

MATERIALS

- 3 [3:4:4] x 100 g balls Rowan Cocoon in M (Polar 801)
- 1 x 50 g ball of Rowan Pure Wool DK in each of A (Kiss 036), B (Marine 008) and C (Tan 054)
- 4 mm and 5.5 mm crochet hooks

ABBREVIATIONS

See page 9.

TENSION

14 stitches and 11 rows to 10 cm (4 in) measured over pattern using 5.5 mm hook and M. Change hook size if necessary to obtain this tension.

KEY   O   ch
               +   dc
               ±   dc worked into front loop only

STITCH DIAGRAM

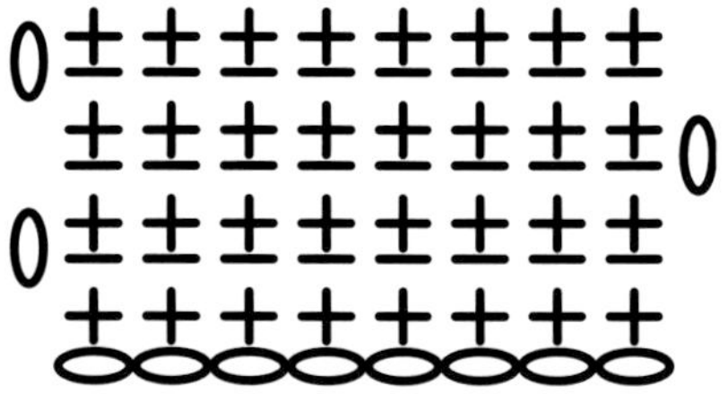

Hat

With 5.5 mm hook and M, make 44 [48:52:56] ch and join with a ss to form a ring.

1st round (RS): 1 ch (does NOT count as st), 1 dc into each ch to end, ss to first dc, turn. 44 [48:52:56] sts.

Now working into front loops only of sts of previous rounds, work in patt as follows:

2nd round: 1 ch (does NOT count as st), 1 dc into each dc to end, ss to first dc, turn.

This round forms patt.

Work in patt for another 10 rounds, ending with RS facing for next round.

4th size only

Next round (RS): 1 ch (does NOT count as st), (1 dc into each of next 6 dc, dc2tog over next 2 dc, 1 dc into each of next 6 dc) 4 times, ss to first dc, turn. 52 sts.

Work 1 round, ending with RS facing for next round.

3RD AND 4TH SIZES ONLY

Next round (RS): 1 ch (does NOT count as st), (1 dc into each of next 5 dc, dc2tog over next 2 dc, 1 dc into each of next 6 dc) 4 times, ss to first dc, turn. 48 sts.

Work 1 round, ending with RS facing for next round.

2nd, 3rd and 4th sizes only

Next round (RS): 1 ch (does NOT count as st), (1 dc into each of next 5 dc, dc2tog over next 2 dc, 1 dc into each of next 5 dc) 4 times, ss to first dc, turn. 44 sts.

Work 1 round, ending with RS facing for next round.

All sizes

Next round (RS): 1 ch (does NOT count as st), (1 dc into each of next 4 dc, dc2tog over next 2 dc, 1 dc into each of next 5 dc) 4 times, ss to first dc, turn. 40 sts.

Work 1 round.

Next round: 1 ch (does NOT count as st), (1 dc into each of next 4 dc, dc2tog over next 2 dc, 1 dc into each of next 4 dc) 4 times, ss to first dc, turn. 36 sts.

Work 1 round.

Next round: 1 ch (does NOT count as st), (1 dc into each of next 3 dc, dc2tog over next 2 dc, 1 dc into each of next 4 dc) 4 times, ss to first dc, turn. 32 sts.

Work 1 round.

Next round: 1 ch (does NOT count as st), (1 dc into each of next 3 dc, dc2tog over next 2 dc, 1 dc into each of next 3 dc) 4 times, ss to first dc, turn. 28 sts.

Work 1 round.

Next round: 1 ch (does NOT count as st), (1 dc into each of next 2 dc, dc2tog over next 2 dc, 1 dc into each of next 3 dc) 4 times, ss to first dc, turn. 24 sts.

Work 1 round.

Next round: 1 ch (does NOT count as st), (1 dc into each of next 2 dc, dc2tog over next 2 dc, 1 dc into each of next 2 dc) 4 times, ss to first dc, turn. 20 sts.

Work 1 round.

Next round: 1 ch (does NOT count as st), (1 dc into next dc, dc2tog over next 2 dc, 1 dc into each of next 2 dc) 4 times, ss to first dc, turn. 16 sts.

Work 1 round.

Next round: 1 ch (does NOT count as st), (1 dc into next dc, dc2tog over next 2 dc, 1 dc into next dc) 4 times, ss to first dc, turn. 12 sts.

Work 1 round.

Next round: 1 ch (does NOT count as st), (dc2tog over next 2 dc, 1 dc into next dc) 4 times, ss to first dc, turn. 8 sts.

Work 1 round.

Next round: 1 ch (does NOT count as st), (dc2tog over next 2 dc) 4 times, ss to first dc, turn. 4 sts.

Work 1 round.

Fasten off.

MAKING UP

As patt consists of dc worked into front loops only of sts of previous rounds, a line is left around work by the 'free' back loops of the sts. Now work contrast stripes around Hat by working into these 'free' loops. Using A, B and C in any order and placing lines at random, attach contrast yarn to one 'free' loop. Using 4 mm hook, work a round of crab st (dc worked from left to right, instead of right to left) around chosen round of Hat, ending with ss to first dc, then fasten off. Take care not to pull yarn too tightly as this could distort the work.

Run a gathering thread around top of last round of Hat, pull up tight and fasten off securely. Using M, A, B and C together, make a 10–12 cm (4–4½ in) long tassel and attach to tip of Hat.

Scarf

With 5.5 mm hook and M, make 15 [16:17:18] ch.

1st row (RS): 1 dc into 2nd ch from hook, 1 dc into each ch to end, turn. 14 [15:16:17] sts.

Now working into front loops only of sts of previous rows, work in patt as follows:

2nd row: 1 ch (does NOT count as st), 1 dc into each dc to end, turn. This row forms patt.

Work in patt until Scarf measures 80 [90:100:110] cm (31¼ [35½:39¼:43¼] in), ending with RS facing for next row.

Fasten off.

MAKING UP

As patt consists of dc worked into front loops only of sts of previous rows, a line is left across work by the 'free' back loops of the sts. Now work contrast stripes across Scarf by working into these 'free' loops. Using A, B and C in any order and placing lines at random, attach contrast yarn to one 'free' loop at edge of Scarf. Using 4 mm hook, work a row of crab st (dc worked from left to right, instead of right to left) along chosen row of Scarf, then fasten off. Take care not to pull yarn too tightly as this could distort the work.

Run a gathering thread along top of last row of Scarf, pull up tight and fasten off securely. Gather foundation ch edge of Scarf in same way. Using M, A, B and C together, make two tassels, each 10–12 cm (4–4½ in) long, and attach to gathered ends of Scarf.

FLARED TUNIC

The angel top takes on a new look with this pretty little flared tunic top! Worked in a shaded yarn that creates the subtle stripes as you crochet, it is simply made in just trebles, and has a useful buttoned opening at the back.

MEASUREMENTS					
age (months)	0–3	3–6	6–12	12–18	
chest	41	46	51	56	cm
	16	18	20	22	in
actual chest	44	50	56	62	cm
	17¼	19½	22	24½	in
length	25	30	35	40	cm
	9¾	11¾	13¾	15¾	in
sleeve seam	13	16	20	26	cm
	5	6¼	7¾	10¼	in

MATERIALS
- 360 [360:480:480] m of multicoloured DK
- 3.5 mm crochet hook
- 1 button

ABBREVIATIONS
See page 9.

TENSION
20 stitches and 9½ rows to 10 cm (4 in) measured over treble fabric using 3.5 mm hook.
Change hook size if necessary to obtain this tension.

STITCH DIAGRAM

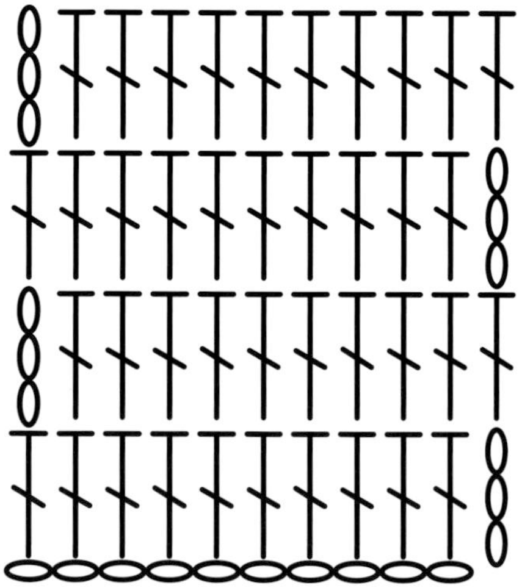

KEY

 o ch

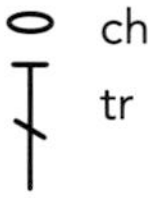

T tr

Shaping note

Decreases

Work all decreases at beg and ends of rows by working 2 sts together. Work dec at beg of row by working "3 ch (does NOT count as st – remember NOT to work into top of this 3 ch when working next row!), 1 tr into next st – 1 st decreased" and work dec at end of row by working "tr2tog over last 2 sts". To decreases several sts at the end of a row, simply turn before the end of the row, leaving the "decreased" sts unworked. To decrease several sts at the beg of a row, ss along top of previous row, working a ss into each "decreased" st and then into what will be first st of next row. Work the "3 ch (counts as first tr)" and then complete the row.

Increases

Work all increases at beg and ends of rows by working 2 sts into one st of previous row. Work inc at beg of row by working "3 ch (counts as first tr), 1 tr into st at base of 3 ch – 1 st increased" and work inc at end of row by working "2 tr into last st".

Body

(worked in one piece to armholes)
With 3.5 mm hook, make 106 [126:146:166] ch.
1st row (RS): 1 tr into 4th ch from hook, 1 tr into each ch to end, turn. 104 [124:144:164] sts.
2nd row: 3 ch (counts as first tr), miss tr at base of 3 ch, 1 tr into each tr to end, working last tr into top of 3 ch at beg of previous row, turn. Last row forms tr fabric.
Work in tr fabric for another 4 rows, ending with RS facing for next row.
7th row: 3 ch (counts as first tr), miss tr at base of 3 ch, 1 tr into each of next 1 [4:7:10] tr, tr2tog over next 2 tr, (1 tr into each of next 12 [14:16:18] tr, tr2tog over next 2 tr) 7 times, 1 tr into each of last 2 [5:8:11] sts, turn. 96 [116:136:156] sts.
Work 3 rows.
11th row: 3 ch (counts as first tr), miss tr at base of 3 ch, 1 tr into each of next 4 [7:10:6] tr, tr2tog over next 2 tr, (1 tr into each of next 10 [12:14:18] tr, tr2tog over next 2 tr) 7 times, 1 tr into each of last 5 [8:11:7] sts, turn. 88 [108:128:148] sts.

2nd, 3rd and 4th sizes only

Work 3 rows.
15th row: 3 ch (counts as first tr), miss tr at base of 3 ch, 1 tr into each of next [3:6:9] tr, tr2tog over next 2 tr, (1 tr into each of next [12:14:16] tr, tr2tog over next 2 tr) 7 times, 1 tr into each of last [4:7:10] sts, turn. [100:120:140] sts.

3rd and 4th sizes only

Work 3 rows.
19th row: 3 ch (counts as first tr), miss tr at base of 3 ch, 1 tr into each of next [2:5] tr, tr2tog over next 2 tr, (1 tr into each of next [14:16] tr, tr2tog over next 2 tr) 7 times, 1 tr into each of last [3:6] sts, turn. [112:132] sts.

4th size only

Work 3 rows.
23rd row: 3 ch (counts as first tr), miss tr at base of 3 ch, 1 tr into each of next 8 tr, tr2tog over next 2 tr, (1 tr into each of next 14 tr, tr2tog over next 2 tr) 7 times, 1 tr into each of last 9 sts, turn. 124 sts.

All sizes

Cont straight until Body measures 15 [19:23:27] cm (6 [7½:9:10½] in).

DIVIDE FOR ARMHOLES

Next row: Patt 19 [22:25:28] sts and turn, leaving rem sts unworked.
Work on this set of 19 [22:25:28] sts only for first back.
Dec 1 st at armhole edge of next 3 [4:5:6] rows. 16 [18:20:22] sts.
Work 4 rows.

SHAPE BACK NECK

Dec 10 [11:12:13] sts at back opening edge of next row. 6 [7:8:9] sts.
Dec 1 st at back neck edge of next row. 5 [6:7:8] sts.

SHAPE SHOULDER

Fasten off.

SHAPE FRONT

Return to last complete row worked, miss next 6 sts, attach yarn to next st and cont as follows:
Next row: Patt 38 [44:50:56] sts and turn, leaving rem sts unworked.
Work on this set of 38 [44:50:56] sts only for front.
Dec 1 st at each end of next 3 [4:5:6] rows. 32 [36:40:44] sts.
Work 1 [1:0:0] row.

SHAPE FRONT NECK

Next row: Patt 9 [10:12:13] sts and turn.
Work on this set of 9 [10:12:13] sts

only for first side of neck.
Dec 1 st at neck edge of next
4 [4:5:5] rows. 5 [6:7:8] sts.

SHAPE SHOULDER
Fasten off.

SHAPE SECOND SIDE OF NECK
Return to last complete row worked
before shaping front neck, miss next
14 [16:16:18] sts, attach yarn to next
tr and cont as follows:
Next row: Patt to end, turn.
9 [10:12:13] sts.
Complete to match first side of neck,
reversing shapings.

SHAPE SECOND BACK
Return to last complete row worked
before dividing for armholes, miss
next 6 sts, attach yarn to next tr and
cont as follows:
Next row: Patt to end, turn.
19 [22:25:28] sts.
Complete to match first back,
reversing shapings.

Sleeves

With 3.5 mm hook, make 26
[28:30:32] ch.
Work first and 2nd rows as given for
Body. 24 [26:28:30] sts.
Cont in tr fabric, inc 1 st at each end
of next 5 [4:2:1] rows, then on foll
2 [4:7:7] alt rows, then on 0 [0:0:2]
foll 3rd rows. 38 [42:46:50] sts.
Cont straight until Sleeve measures
13 [16:20:26] cm (5 [6¼:7¼:10¼] in).

SHAPE TOP
Dec 3 sts at each end of next row.
32 [36:40:44] sts.
Dec 1 st at each end of next 6 [7:8:9]

rows. 20 [22:24:26] sts.
Fasten off.

Making up

Join shoulder seams. Join centre
back seam, leaving seam open for
6 cm (2¼ in) at neck edge.

NECK EDGING
With RS facing and using 3.5 mm
hook, rejoin yarn at right back neck
edge at top of back opening,
1 ch (does NOT count as st), work
1 round of dc evenly down right back

opening edge, up left back opening
edge, then around entire neck edge,
ending with ss to first dc, turn.
Next round: 1 ch (does NOT count
as st), 1 dc into each dc to top of left
side of back opening, 4 ch (to make
a button loop), 1 dc into each dc, ss
to 1st dc.
Fasten off.

Join sleeve seams. Insert sleeves
into armholes, matching centre of
last row to shoulder seam and top of
sleeve seam to centre of sts missed
at underarm. Sew on button.

FURRY HAT, BOOTS AND MITTS

A classic but simple fur, or loop, stitch pattern has been used to create this fun set. Worked in a pure wool yarn, the hat has cosy earflaps to keep out chill winds and the little pull-on boots and mitts will keep little toes and hands warm too.

MEASUREMENTS					
age (months)	0–3	3–6	6–12	12–18	
HAT					
width around head	33	36	39	42	cm
	13	14	15¼	16½	in
BOOTS					
length of foot	8	9	10	11	cm
	3	3½	4	4¼	in
MITTS					
width around hand	10	11	12	13	cm
	4	4¼	4¾	5	in

MATERIALS
• 2 [2:3:3] x 50 g balls of Rowan Pure Wool DK in Enamel 013
• 3.5 mm crochet hook

ABBREVIATIONS
• **loop 1** – insert hook into next st, form loop of yarn around first finger of left hand and draw both strands of this looped yarn through st, yarn over hook and draw through all 3 loops on hook.
See also page 9.

TENSION
20 stitches and 24 rows to 10 cm (4 in) measured over pattern using 3.5 mm hook.
Change hook size if necessary to obtain this tension.

STITCH DIAGRAM

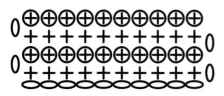

KEY
o ch
+ dc
⊕ loop 1

Hat

With 3.5 mm hook, make 66 [72:78:84] ch and join with a ss to form a ring.

1st round (RS): 1 ch (does NOT count as st), 1 dc into each ch to end, ss to first dc, turn. 66 [72:78:84] sts.

2nd round: 1 ch (does NOT count as st), loop 1 into each dc to end, ss to first st, turn.

3rd round: 1 ch (does NOT count as st), 1 dc into each st to end, ss to first st, turn.

2nd and 3rd rounds form patt.

Cont in patt until Hat measures 8 [9:9:10] cm (3 [3½:3½:4] in), ending with RS facing for next round.

SHAPE TOP

1st round (RS): 1 ch (does NOT count as st), (dc2tog over next 2 sts, 1 dc into each of next 4 sts) 11 [12:13:14] times, ss to first st, turn. 55 [60:65:70] sts. Work 3 rounds.

5th round: 1 ch (does NOT count as st), (dc2tog over next 2 sts, 1 dc into each of next 3 sts) 11 [12:13:14] times, ss to first st, turn. 44 [48:52:56] sts. Work 3 rounds.

9th round: 1 ch (does NOT count as st), (dc2tog over next 2 sts, 1 dc into each of next 2 sts) 11 [12:13:14] times, ss to first st, turn. 33 [36:39:42] sts. Work 3 rounds.

13th round: 1 ch (does NOT count as st), (dc2tog over next 2 sts, 1 dc into next st) 11 [12:13:14] times, ss to first st, turn. 22 [24:26:28] sts. Work 1 round.

15th round: 1 ch (does NOT count as st), (dc2tog over next 2 sts) 11 [12:13:14] times, ss to first st, turn. 11 [12:13:14] sts. Work 1 round.

17th round: 1 ch (does NOT count as st), (dc2tog over next 2 sts) 5 [6:6:7] times, (1 dc into last st) 1 [0:1:0] times, ss to first st, do NOT turn. 6 [6:7:7] sts.

18th round: 1 ch (does NOT count as st), 1 dc into each of next 6 [6:7:7] dc, do NOT turn and do NOT close round with a ss.

Rep last round 4 times more, ending last round with ss to next dc.

Fasten off.

MAKING UP

Run a gathering thread around top of last round of Hat, pull up tight and fasten off securely.

EARFLAPS (MAKE 2)

With RS facing and 3.5 mm hook, miss first 8 [9:10:11] sts of foundation ch, attach yarn to next st of foundation ch and cont as follows:

1st row (RS): 1 ch (does NOT count as st), 1 dc into st where yarn was attached, 1 dc into each of next 11 sts of foundation ch, turn. 12 sts.

2nd row: 1 ch (does NOT count as st), 1 dc into each dc to end, turn.

3rd and 4th rows: As 2nd row.

5th row: 1 ch (does NOT count as st), dc2tog over first 2 dc, 1 dc into each dc to last 2 dc, dc2tog over last 2 dc, turn. 10 sts.

6th to 8th rows: As 2nd row.

9th row: As 5th row. 8 sts.

10th row: As 2nd row.

11th to 13th rows: As 5th row. 2 sts.

Fasten off.

Return to foundation ch edge of Hat, miss centre front 26 [30:34:38] sts, attach yarn to next st of foundation ch edge and complete second Earflap to match first by working first to 13th rows.

LOWER EDGING AND TIES

With RS facing and 3.5 mm hook, attach yarn to centre back point of foundation ch edge of Hat, 1 ch (does NOT count as st), work evenly in dc along foundation ch edge to first Earflap, then down first side of Earflap to fasten-off point, make 40 ch, 1 dc into 2nd ch from hook, 1 dc into each ch back to fasten-off point of Earflap (to make first Tie), cont in dc around rest of lower edge of Hat and other Earflap, making a second Tie in same way at point of other Earflap, and ending with ss to first dc.

Fasten off.

If desired, snip each loop of patt to create fur-like effect.

Boots (MAKE 2 ALIKE)

With 3.5 mm hook, make 9 [10:11:12] ch.

1st round (RS): 2 dc into 2nd ch from hook, 1 dc into each of next 6 [7:8:9] ch, 4 dc into last ch, working back along other side of foundation ch: 1 dc into each of next 6 [7:8:9] ch, 2 dc into last ch (this is same ch as used for first 2 dc), ss to first dc, turn. 20 [22:24:26] sts.

2nd round: 1 ch (does NOT count as st), 2 dc into each of first 2 dc, 1 dc into each of next 6 [7:8:9] dc, 2 dc into each of next 4 dc, 1 dc into each of next 6 [7:8:9] dc, 2 dc into each of last 2 dc, ss to first dc, turn.

28 [30:32:34] sts.

3rd round: 1 ch (does NOT count as st), *(1 dc into next dc, 2 dc into next dc) twice, 1 dc into each of next 6 [7:8:9] dc, (2 dc into next dc, 1 dc into next dc) twice, rep from * once more, ss to first dc, turn. 36 [38:40:42] sts.

4th round: 1 ch (does NOT count as st), *(1 dc into each of next 2 dc, 2 dc into next dc) twice, 1 dc into each of next 6 [7:8:9] dc, (2 dc into

next dc, 1 dc into each of next 2 dc) twice, rep from * once more, ss to first dc, turn. 44 [46:48:50] sts. These 4 rounds complete base of Boot.

5th round: 1 ch (does NOT count as st), 1 dc into back loop only of each dc to end, ss to first dc, turn.

6th round: 1 ch (does NOT count as st), loop 1 into each dc to end, ss to first dc, turn.

7th round: 1 ch (does NOT count

as st), 1 dc into each st to end, ss to first dc, turn.

8th round: As 6th round.

9th round: 1 ch (does NOT count as st), dc2tog over first 2 sts, 1 dc into each st to last 2 sts, dc2tog over last 2 sts, ss to first st, turn. 42 [44:46:48] sts.

Rep last 2 rounds twice more. 38 [40:42:44] sts.

14th round: As 6th round.

15th round: Fold Boot flat so that

tops of last round meet and RS is inside, 1 ch (does NOT count as st), taking care not to catch loops in sts, work 1 dc into each of first 6 sts enclosing last 6 sts of round in these sts (to join seam on top of foot – 12 sts decreased), open out work again and turn RS out, 1 dc into each of next 26 [28:30:32] sts, ss to top of first of these dc, turn. 26 [28:30:32] sts.

16th round: As 6th round.
17th round: As 9th round.
24 [26:28:30] sts.
Now working in rows, not rounds, cont as follows:
18th row (WS): 1 ch (does NOT count as st), loop 1 into each dc to end, turn.
19th row: 1 ch (does NOT count as st), dc2tog over first 2 sts, 1 dc into each st to last 2 sts, dc2tog over last 2 sts, turn. 22 [24:26:28] sts.
Rep last 2 rows once more.
20 [22:24:26] sts.
22nd row: As 18th row.
23rd row: 1 ch (does NOT count as st), 1 dc into each st to end, turn.
24th row: As 18th row.
Fasten off.

MAKING UP
With RS facing and 3.5 mm hook, attach yarn at base of front split (point where work stops being rounds and starts being rows), 1 ch (does NOT count as st), work evenly in dc around entire upper opening edge of Boot, ending with ss to first dc.
Fasten off.

If desired, snip each loop of patt to create fur-like effect.

Mitts (MAKE 2 ALIKE)

With 3.5 mm hook, make 16 [18:20:22] ch and join with a ss to form a ring.
1st round (RS): 1 ch (does NOT count as st), 1 dc into each ch to end, ss to first dc, turn. 16 [18:20:22] sts.
2nd round: 1 ch (does NOT count as st), 1 dc into each dc to end, ss to first st, turn.
3rd round: 1 ch (does NOT count as st), 2 dc into first dc, 1 dc into each of next 6 [7:8:9] dc, 2 dc into each of next 2 dc, 1 dc into each of next 6 [7:8:9] dc, 2 dc into last dc, ss to first st, turn. 20 [22:24:26] sts.
4th round: 1 ch (does NOT count as st), loop 1 into each dc to end, ss to first st, turn.
5th round: 1 ch (does NOT count as st), 1 dc into each st to end, ss to first st, turn.
4th and 5th rounds form patt.
Cont in patt for another 9 [9:11:11] rounds, ending with RS facing for next round.

SHAPE TOP
Next round: 1 ch (does NOT count as st), (dc2tog over next 2 sts, 1 dc into each of next 6 [7:8:9] sts, dc2tog over next 2 sts) twice, ss to first st, turn. 16 [18:20:22] sts.
Work 1 round.
Next round: 1 ch (does NOT count as st), (dc2tog over next 2 sts, 1 dc into each of next 4 [5:6:7] sts, dc2tog over next 2 sts) twice, ss to first st, turn. 12 [14:16:18] sts.
Work 1 round.
Next round: 1 ch (does NOT count as st), (dc2tog over next 2 sts, 1 dc

into each of next 2 [3:4:5] sts, dc2tog over next 2 sts) twice, ss to first st, turn. 8 [10:12:14] sts.
Work 1 round.
Fasten off.

MAKING UP
Join top seam.
If desired, snip each loop of patt to create fur-like effect.

ENVELOPE NECK SWEATER

Made using just trebles and double crochet, this little sweater has a wide envelope neck so it is easy to get on and off even the wriggliest baby! Worked in a hand-dyed yarn that is mainly cotton, the clever shaded colour effect adds interest without the need for complicated stitches.

MEASUREMENTS					
age (months)	0–3	3–6	6–12	12–18	
chest	41	46	51	56	cm
	16	18	20	22	in
actual chest	45	52	58	64	cm
	17¾	20½	22¾	25	in
length	21	25	29	33	cm
	8¼	9¾	11½	13	in
sleeve seam	13	16	20	26	cm
	5	6¼	7¾	10¼	in

MATERIALS
- 3 [4:4:5] x 50 g hanks of Colinette Banyan in Fire 71
- 3 mm and 3.5 mm crochet hooks

ABBREVIATIONS
See page 9.

TENSION
19 stitches and 9 rows to 10 cm (4 in) measured over treble fabric using 3.5 mm hook.
Change hook size if necessary to obtain this tension.

STITCH DIAGRAM

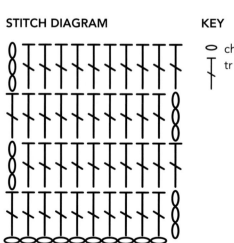

KEY
⊙ ch
┼ tr

Shaping note

Decreases

Work all decreases at beg and ends of rows by working 2 sts together. Work dec at beg of row by working "3 ch (does NOT count as st – remember NOT to work into top of this 3 ch when working next row!), 1 tr into next st – 1 st decreased" and work dec at end of row by working "tr2tog over last 2 sts". To decreases several sts at the end of row, simply turn before the end of the row, leaving the "decreased" sts unworked. To decrease several sts at the beg of a row, ss along top of previous row, working a ss into each "decreased" st and then into what will be first st of next row. Work the "3 ch (counts as first tr)" and then complete the row.

Increases

Work all increases at beg and ends of rows by working 2 sts into one st of previous row. Work inc at beg of row by working "3 ch (counts as first tr), 1 tr into st at base of 3 ch – 1 st increased" and work inc at end of row by working "2 tr into last st".

Back

With 3 mm hook, make 44 [50:56:62] ch.
1st row (RS): 1 dc into 2nd ch from hook, 1 dc into each ch to end, turn. 43 [49:55:61] sts.
2nd row: 1 ch (does NOT count as st), 1 dc into each dc to end, turn.
Rep last row twice more.
Change to 3.5 mm hook.

5th row: 3 ch (counts as first tr), miss dc at base of 3 ch, 1 tr into each dc to end, turn.
6th row: 3 ch (counts as first tr), miss tr at base of 3 ch, 1 tr into each tr to end, working last tr into top of 3 ch at beg of previous row, turn.
Last row forms tr fabric.
Work in tr fabric until Back measures 11 [14:17:20] cm (4¼ [5½:6½:7¾] in).

SHAPE ARMHOLES

Dec 3 sts at each end of next row. 37 [43:49:55] sts.
Dec 1 st at each end of next 3 [4:5:6] rows. 31 [35:39:43] sts.**
Work 3 rows.

SHAPE BACK NECK

Next row: Patt 7 sts and turn, leaving rem sts unworked.
Work on this set of 7 sts only for first side of neck.
Dec 1 st at neck edge of next 5 rows. 2 sts.
Fasten off.
Place marker along armhole edge 4 rows down from fasten-off point.

SHAPE SECOND SIDE OF NECK

Return to last complete row worked before shaping neck, miss next 17 [21:25:29] sts, attach yarn to next tr and cont as follows:
Next row: Patt to end, turn. 7 sts.
Complete to match first side of neck, reversing shapings.

Front

Work as given for Back to **.

SHAPE FRONT NECK

Next row: Patt 6 sts and turn, leaving rem sts unworked.
Work on this set of 6 sts only for first side of neck.
Dec 1 st at neck edge of next 4 rows. 2 sts.
Fasten off.
Place marker on armhole edge at top of last row.

SHAPE SECOND SIDE OF NECK

Return to last complete row worked before shaping neck, miss next 19 [23:27:31] sts, attach yarn to next

BACK AND FRONT

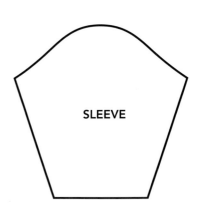

SLEEVE

tr and cont as follows:
Next row: Patt to end, turn. 6 sts.
Complete to match first side of neck,
reversing shapings.

Sleeves

With 3 mm hook, make 24 [26:28:
30] ch.
Work 1st to 5th rows as given for
Back (remembering to change to
3.50 mm hook after 4th row).
23 [25:27:29] sts.
Cont in tr fabric, inc 1 st at each end
of next 7 [8:9:10] rows. 37 [41:45:
49] sts.
Cont straight until Sleeve measures
13 [16:20:26] cm (5 [6¼:7¾:10¼] in).

SHAPE TOP
Dec 3 sts at each end of next row.
31 [35:39:43] sts.
Dec 1 st at each end of next 5 [6:7:8]
rows. 21 [23:25:27] sts.
Fasten off.

Making up

FRONT NECK EDGING
With RS facing and using 3 mm
hook, rejoin yarn at top of left front
neck, 1 ch (does NOT count as st),
work 1 row of dc evenly around
entire front neck edge, turn.
Next row: 1 ch (does NOT count as
st), 2 dc into first dc, 1 dc into each
dc to last dc, 2 dc into last dc.
Fasten off.

BACK NECK EDGING
Work as given for Front Neck Edging.
Arrange back neck edge over front
so that markers match and sew row-

end edges of Back and Back Neck
Edging and Front and Front Neck
Edging together along armhole
edges. Join side seams. Join sleeve

seams. Insert sleeves into armholes,
matching centre of top of last row of
sleeves to marked points.

HAT, SCARF AND BAG

This pretty hat, scarf and bag set will make any little girl feel really grown up! The ruffle effect is simply created by working groups of trebles that form pretty shells. Made in a hand-dyed yarn, the subtle colour effect adds to the finished look.

MEASUREMENTS					
age (months)	0–3	3–6	6–12	12–18	
HAT					
width around head	33	35	38	41	cm
	13	13¾	15	16	in
SCARF					
width	7	7	7	7	cm
	2¾	2¾	2¾	2¾	in
length (approximate)	70	79	89	98	cm
	27½	31	35	38½	in

MATERIALS
- 2 [2:3:3] x 110 g hanks of Colinette Jitterbug in Marble 88
- 2.5 mm crochet hook

ABBREVIATIONS
See page 9.

TENSION
22 stitches and 11 rows to 10 cm (4 in) measured over tr fabric using 2.5 mm hook.
Change hook size if necessary to obtain this tension.

STITCH DIAGRAM

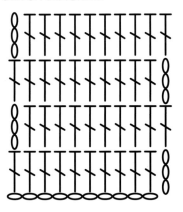

KEY

o ch

✝ tr

Hat

With 2.5 mm hook, make 4 ch.
1st round (RS): 11 [12:13:14] tr into 4th ch from hook, ss to top of 3 ch at beg of round, do NOT turn. 12 [13:14:15] sts.
2nd round: 3 ch (counts as first tr), 1 tr into same place as ss at end of previous round, 2 tr into each tr to end, ss to top of 3 ch at beg of round, do NOT turn. 24 [26:28:30] sts.
3rd round: 3 ch (counts as first tr), 1 tr into same place as ss at end of previous round, *1 tr into next tr**, 2 tr into next tr, rep from * to end, ending last rep at **, ss to top of 3 ch at beg of round, do NOT turn. 36 [39:42:45] sts.
4th round: 3 ch (counts as first tr), 1 tr into same place as ss at end of previous round, *1 tr into each of next 2 tr**, 2 tr into next tr, rep from * to end, ending last rep at **, ss to top of 3 ch at beg of round, do NOT turn. 48 [52:56:60] sts.
5th round: 3 ch (counts as first tr), 1 tr into same place as ss at end of previous round, *1 tr into each of next 3 tr**, 2 tr into next tr, rep from * to end, ending last rep at **, ss to top of 3 ch at beg of round, do NOT turn. 60 [65:70:75] sts.
6th round: 3 ch (counts as first tr), miss st at base of 3 ch, 1 tr into each of tr to end, ss to top of 3 ch at beg of round, do NOT turn.
7th round: 3 ch (counts as first tr), 1 tr into same place as ss at end of previous round, *1 tr into each of next 4 tr**, 2 tr into next tr, rep from * to end, ending last rep at **, ss to top of 3 ch at beg of round, do NOT turn. 72 [78:84:90] sts.

Now rep 6th round 7 [7:8:8] times more.

EDGING

1st round: 1 ch (does NOT count as st), 1 dc into each st to end, ss to first dc.
2nd round: As 1st round.
3rd round: 3 ch (counts as first tr), (2 tr, 1 ch and 3 tr) into same place as ss at end of previous round, *miss 2 dc**, (3 tr, 1 ch and 3 tr) into next dc, rep from * to end, ending last rep at **, ss to top of 3 ch at beg of round.
4th round: Ss across and into first ch sp, 3 ch (counts as first tr), 8 tr into same ch sp, *miss 6 tr**, 9 tr into next ch sp, rep from * to end, ending last rep at **, ss to top of 3 ch at beg of round.
Fasten off.

Scarf

With 2.5 mm hook, make 141 [162:183:204] ch.
1st round (RS): 3 tr into 4th ch from hook, 1 tr into each ch to last ch, 8 tr into last ch, now working back along other side of foundation ch: 1 tr into each ch to ch at base of 3 ch at beg of round, 4 tr into same ch as used for 3 tr at beg of round, ss to top of 3 ch at beg of round, do NOT turn. 288 [330:372:414] sts.
2nd round: 3 ch (counts as first tr), (2 tr, 1 ch and 3 tr) into same place as ss at end of previous round, *miss 2 tr**, (3 tr, 1 ch and 3 tr) into next tr, rep from * to end, ending last rep at **, ss to top of 3 ch at beg of round.
3rd round: Ss across and into first ch sp, 3 ch (counts as first tr), 8 tr into

same ch sp, *miss 6 tr**, 9 tr into next ch sp, rep from * to end, ending last rep at **, ss to top of 3 ch at beg of round.
Fasten off.

Bag

MAIN SECTION

With 2.5 mm hook, make 33 ch.
1st round (RS): 1 tr into 4th ch from hook, 1 tr into each of next 28 ch, 4 tr into last ch, now working back along other side of foundation ch: 1 tr into each of next 28 ch, 2 tr into same ch as used for tr at beg of round, ss to top of 3 ch at beg of round, do NOT turn. 64 sts.
2nd round: 3 ch (counts as first tr), 1 tr into st at base of 3 ch, 1 tr into each of next 30 tr, 2 tr into each of next 2 tr, 1 tr into each of next 30 tr, 2 tr into last tr, ss to top of 3 ch at beg of round, do NOT turn. 68 sts.
3rd round: 3 ch (counts as first tr), 1 tr into st at base of 3 ch, 1 tr into each of next 32 tr, 2 tr into each of next 2 tr, 1 tr into each of next 32 tr, 2 tr into last tr, ss to top of 3 ch at beg of round, do NOT turn. 72 sts.
4th round: 3 ch (counts as first tr), 1 tr into st at base of 3 ch, 1 tr into each of next 34 tr, 2 tr into each of next 2 tr, 1 tr into each of next 34 tr, 2 tr into last tr, ss to top of 3 ch at beg of round, do NOT turn. 76 sts.
5th round: 3 ch (counts as first tr), miss st at base of 3 ch, 1 tr into each tr to end, ss to top of 3 ch at beg of round, do NOT turn.
6th to 15th rounds: As 5th round.
16th round: 3 ch (counts as first tr), miss st at base of 3 ch, *(tr2tog over next 2 tr, 1 tr into next tr) 3 times,

tr2tog over next 2 tr, 1 tr into each of next 14 tr, tr2tog over next 2 tr, (1 tr into next tr, tr2tog over next 2 tr) 3 times*, 1 tr into each of next 2 tr, rep from * to * once more, 1 tr into last tr, ss to top of 3 ch at beg of round, turn. 60 sts.

17th round (WS): 1 ch (does NOT count as st), 1 dc into each st to end, ss to first dc, turn.

18th round: 1 ch (does NOT count as st), working into back loops only of sts of previous round: 1 dc into each dc to end, ss to first dc, turn.

19th round: 1 ch (does NOT count as st), 1 dc into each st to end, ss to first dc, do NOT turn

20th to 31st rounds: As 19th round. Fasten off.

TOP FLOUNCE

With RS facing and with upper opening edge toward you (so that WS of flounce sits against RS of lower section of bag), attach yarn to rem free loop of one dc at side edge of 17th round, 1 ch (does NOT count as st), 1 dc into each dc of 17th round, ss to first dc, do NOT turn. 60 sts.

2nd round: 3 ch (counts as first tr), (2 tr, 1 ch and 3 tr) into same place as ss at end of previous round, *miss 2 dc**, (3 tr, 1 ch and 3 tr) into next dc, rep from * to end, ending last rep at **, ss to top of 3 ch at beg of round.

3rd round: Ss across and into first ch sp, 3 ch (counts as first tr), 8 tr into same ch sp, *miss 6 tr**, 9 tr into next ch sp, rep from * to end, ending last rep at **, ss to top of 3 ch at beg of round.
Fasten off.

HANDLE

With 2.5 mm hook, make 9 ch and join with a ss to form a ring.

1st round (RS): 1 ch (does NOT count as st), 1 dc into each ch to end, do NOT close ring with a ss and do NOT turn. 9 sts.

2nd round: 1 dc into each dc of previous round.

Rep last round (thereby making a spiralling tube of dc) until Handle measures 26 cm (10¼ in).

Fasten off.

Making up

Fold last round of Main Section to inside around opening edge, so that top of last round meets top of last tr round. Slip stitch in place. Using photograph as a guide, sew ends of Handle inside upper edge of Bag.

COLOUR BLOCK TUNIC AND JACKET

Bold blocks of colour are combined with a simple textured stitch to create this tunic or jacket. The stitch is really easy to work as it is just a variation of plain double crochet fabric, and the classic cotton yarn means it will be soft and comfortable for baby to wear.

MEASUREMENTS					
age (months)	0–3	3–6	6–12	12–18	
chest	41	46	51	56	cm
	16	18	20	22	in
actual chest	48	53	58	63	cm
	19	20¾	22¾	24¾	in
length	26	30	34	38	cm
	10¼	11¾	13¼	15	in
sleeve seam	13	16	20	26	cm
	5	6¼	7¾	10¼	in

MATERIALS
• 3.5 mm and 4 mm crochet hooks
Tunic
• Rowan Handknit Cotton (50 g balls): 1 [2:2:2] balls in A (Raspberry 356), 1 [2:2:2] balls in B (Delphinium 334), and 1 [2:2:2] balls in C (Aubergine 348)
• 1 button
Jacket
• Rowan Handknit Cotton (50 g balls): 1 [2:2:2] balls in A (Raffia 330), 1 [2:2:2] balls in B (Pesto 344), and 1 [2:2:2] balls in C (Gooseberry 219)
• Open-ended zip to fit

ABBREVIATIONS
See page 9

TENSION
16 stitches and 16 rows to 10 cm (4 in) measured over pattern using 4 mm hook.
Change hook size if necessary to obtain this tension.

STITCH DIAGRAM

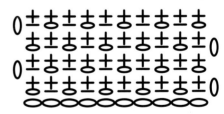

KEY
o ch
± dc in back loop
ꝷ dc in front loop

Shaping note

Decreases

Work all decreases at beg and ends of rows by working 2 sts together. Work dec at beg of row by working "1 ch (does NOT count as st), dc2tog over next 2 sts – 1 st decreased" and work dec at end of row by working "dc2tog over last 2 sts". As patt consists of dc worked alternately into front and back of sts of previous row, place the sts that make up the "dc2tog" according to the patt.
To decrease several sts at the end of a row, simply turn before the end of the row, leaving the "decreased" sts unworked. To decrease several sts at the beg of a row, ss along top of previous row, working a ss into each "decreased" st and then into what will be first st of next row. Work the "1 ch (does NOT count as st) and a dc into st at base of this 1 ch" and then complete the row.

Increases

Work all increases at beg and ends of rows by working 2 sts into one st of previous row. Work inc at beg of row by working "1 ch (does NOT count as st), 2 dc into st at base of 1 ch – 1 st increased" and work inc at end of row by working "2 dc into last st".

Tunic back

With 3.5 mm hook and A, make 39 [43:47:51] ch.
1st row (RS): 1 dc into 2nd ch from hook, 1 dc into each ch to end, turn. 38 [42:46:50] sts.

2nd row: 1 ch (does NOT count as st), 1 dc into each dc to end, turn. Change to 4 mm hook.
Join in B and now work in patt as follows:
3rd row: Using B, 1 ch (does NOT count as st), 1 dc into back loop only of dc at base of 1 ch, (1 dc into front loop only of next dc, 1 dc into back loop only of next dc) 9 [10:11:12] times, using A, (1 dc into front loop only of next dc, 1 dc into back loop only of next dc) 9 [10:11:12] times, 1 dc into front loop only of last dc, turn.
4th row: Using A, 1 ch (does NOT count as st), 1 dc into back loop only of dc at base of 1 ch, (1 dc into front loop only of next dc, 1 dc into back loop only of next dc) 9 [10:11:12] times, using B, (1 dc into front loop only of next dc, 1 dc into back loop only of next dc) 9 [10:11:12] times, 1 dc into front loop only of last dc, turn.
Last 2 rows form patt and place colours for first section.
Cont as set until Back measures 10 [12:14:15] cm (4 [4¾:5½:6] in), ending with RS facing for next row.
Break off A and join in C.
Using C instead of A, cont straight until Back measures 16 [18:20:23] cm (6¼ [7:7¾:9] in), ending with RS facing for next row.
Break off B and join in A.**
Using A instead of B, cont straight until Back measures 20 [24:28:32] cm (7¾ [9½:11:12½] in), ending with RS facing for next row.

Divide for back opening

Next row: Patt 19 [21:23:25] sts and turn, leaving rem sts unworked. Work on this set of sts only for first side of neck.
Cont straight until Back measures 26 [30:34:38] cm (10¼ [11¾:13¼: 15] in), ending with RS facing for next row.

SHAPE SHOULDER

Fasten off, placing marker 11 [12:13:14] sts in from side seam edge to denote back neck.

Return to last complete row worked before dividing for back opening, attach C to next dc, 1 ch (does NOT count as st), patt to end. 19 [21:23:25] sts.
Complete to match first side.

Tunic front

Work as given for Back to **.
Using A instead of B, cont straight until 8 [8:10:10] rows less have been worked than on Back to fasten-off point, ending with RS facing for next row.

SHAPE FRONT NECK

Next row: Patt 16 [17:19:20] sts and turn, leaving rem sts unworked.
Work on this set of 16 [17:19:20] sts only for first side of neck.
Dec 1 st at neck edge of next 4 rows, then on 1 [1:2:2] foll alt rows. 11 [12:13:14] sts.
Work 1 row, ending with RS facing for next row. Fasten off.

Return to last complete row worked before shaping neck, miss centre 6 [8:8:10] sts, attach C to next dc, 1 ch (does NOT count as st), patt to end. 16 [17:19:20] sts.

Complete to match first side, reversing shapings.

Left sleeve

With 3.50 mm hook and A, make 20 [22:24:26] ch.
Work first and 2nd rows as given for Back. 19 [21:23:25] sts.
Change to 4 mm hook.
Break off A and join in C.
Now work in patt as follows:
3rd row: 1 ch (does NOT count as st), 1 dc into back loop only of dc at base of 1 ch, *1 dc into front loop only of next dc, 1 dc into back loop only of next dc, rep from * to end, turn.
4th row: 1 ch (does NOT count as st), 2 dc into dc at base of 1 ch – 1 st increased, * 1 dc into back loop only of next dc, 1 dc into front loop only of next dc, rep from * to last 2 sts, 1 dc into back loop only of next dc, 2 dc into last dc – 1 st increased, turn.
Last 2 rows form patt and set increases.
Cont in patt, inc 1 st at each end of next [2nd:2nd:3rd] and 6 [5:3:6] foll alt [alt:alt:3rd] rows, then on 0 [2:5:3] foll 0 [3rd:3rd:4th] rows, taking inc sts into patt. 35 [39:43:47] sts.
Cont straight until Sleeve measures 13 [16:20:26] cm (5 [6¼:7¾:10¼] in).
Fasten off.

Right sleeve

Work as given for Left Sleeve, but using B in place of C.

Making up

Join shoulder seams.

NECK EDGING
With RS facing, using 3.5 mm hook and A, attach yarn at top of left back opening edge, 1 ch (does NOT count as st), work 1 row of dc evenly around neck edge to top of right back opening edge, 5 ch (to make button loop), ss to last dc.
Fasten off.
Mark points along side seam edges 11 [12:13:14] cm (4¼ [4¾:5:5½] in) to each side of the shoulder seams and sew Sleeves to Back and Front between these points. Join side and sleeve seams. Sew on button.

Jacket back

Work as given for Back of Tunic to **.
Using A instead of B, cont straight until Back measures 26 [30:34:38] cm

(10¼ [11¾:13¼:15] in), ending with RS facing for next row.
Fasten off, placing markers 11 [12:13:14] sts in from side seam edges to denote back neck.

Left front

With 3.50 mm hook and A, make 20 [22:24:26] ch.
Work first and 2nd rows as given for Back. 19 [21:23:25] sts.
Change to 4 mm hook.
Break off A and join in B.
Now work in patt as follows:
3rd row: 1 ch (does NOT count as st), 1 dc into back loop only of dc at base of 1 ch, * 1 dc into front loop only of next dc, 1 dc into back loop only of next dc, rep from * to end, turn.
4th row: 1 ch (does NOT count as st), 1 dc into front loop only of dc at base of 1 ch, * 1 dc into back loop only of next dc, 1 dc into front loop only of next dc, rep from * to end, turn.
Last 2 rows form patt.
Cont as set until Left Front measures

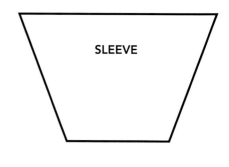

BACK AND FRONT

SLEEVE

16 [18:20:23] cm (6¼ [7:7¾:9] in), ending with RS facing for next row. Break off B and join in A.
Cont straight until 8 [8:10:10] rows less have been worked than on Back to fasten-off point, ending with RS facing for next row.

SHAPE NECK
Dec 3 [4:4:5] sts at end of next row. 16 [17:19:20] sts.
Dec 1 st at neck edge of next 4 rows, then on 1 [1:2:2] foll alt rows. 11 [12:13:14] sts.
Work 1 row, ending with RS facing for next row.
Fasten off.

Right front

With 3.5 mm hook and A, make 20 [22:24:26] ch.
Work first and 2nd rows as given for Back. 19 [21:23:25] sts.
Change to 4 mm hook.
Now work in patt as follows:
3rd row: 1 ch (does NOT count as st), 1 dc into front loop only of dc at base of 1 ch, * 1 dc into back loop only of next dc, 1 dc into front loop only of next dc, rep from * to end, turn.
4th row: 1 ch (does NOT count as st), 1 dc into back loop only of dc at base of 1 ch, * 1 dc into front loop only of next dc, 1 dc into back loop only of next dc, rep from * to end, turn.
Last 2 rows form patt.

Cont as set until Right Front measures 10 [12:14:15] cm (4 [4¾:5½:6] in), ending with RS facing for next row.
Break off A and join in C.
Complete to match Left Front, reversing shapings.

Sleeves

Work as given for Sleeves of Tunic.

Making up

Join shoulder seams.

FRONT AND NECK EDGING
With RS facing, using 3.5 mm hook and A, attach yarn at base of right front opening edge, 1 ch (does NOT count as st), work 1 row of dc evenly up right front opening edge, around entire neck edge, and down left front opening edge to foundation ch edge, working 3 dc into neck corner points, turn.
Next row: 1 ch (does NOT count as st), 1 dc into each dc to end, working 3 dc into neck corner points and missing dc as required around neck edge to ensure edging lies flat.
Fasten off.

Mark points along side seam edges 11 [12:13:14] cm (4¼ [4¾:5:5½] in) to each side of shoulder seams and sew Sleeves to Back and Fronts between these points. Join side and sleeve seams. Insert zip into front opening.

BLAZER

Styled to echo a classic nautical blazer, this little double-breasted jacket is made in a machine washable wool and cotton mixture yarn. The simple textured stitch combines just trebles and double crochet and the jolly brass buttons complete the stylish look.

MEASUREMENTS					
age (months)	0–3	3–6	6–12	12–18	
chest	41	46	51	56	cm
	16	18	20	22	in
actual chest	47	54	61	68	cm
	18½	21¼	24	26¾	in
length	23	27	31	35	cm
	9	10½	12¼	13¾	in
sleeve seam	12	15	19	23	cm
	4¾	6	7½	9	in

MATERIALS
- 4 [4:5:5] x 50 g balls of Rowan Wool Cotton in French Navy 909
- 3.5 mm crochet hook
- 4 buttons

ABBREVIATIONS
See page 9.

TENSION
17 stitches and 14 rows to 10 cm (4 in) measured over pattern using 3.5 mm hook.
Change hook size if necessary to obtain this tension.

STITCH DIAGRAM

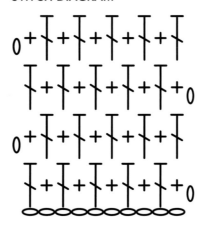

KEY
- ○ ch
- + dc
- T tr

Shaping note

Decreases

To dec 1 st at beg of row, work: 1 ss into each of first 2 sts, make appropriate turning ch – which may or may not count as st depending on point in patt, if it DOES count as a st, miss st at base of turning ch, but if it DOES NOT count as st, work appropriate st into st at base of turning ch.

To dec 1 st at end of row, simply turn 1 st before end of row, leaving decreased st unworked.

To work a multiple dec at beg of row, break and fasten off yarn. Miss the appropriate number of sts and rejoin yarn to next st, make appropriate turning ch (depending on point in patt) and complete row. To work a multiple dec at the end of a row, simply turn the required number of sts before the end of the row, leaving the "decreased" sts unworked.

Increases

Work all increases at beg and ends of rows by working 2 sts into one st of previous row. Remember patt alternates between a dc and a tr and work sts accordingly. If first st of new row should be a dc, inc will be "3 ch (counts as tr), 1 dc into st at base of 3 ch". If first st of new row should be a tr, inc will be "1 ch (does NOT count as st, (1 dc and 1 tr) into st at base of 1 ch".

Pattern note

As there are no edgings on this garment, it is important to keep the outer finished edges neat.

Body

(worked in one piece to armholes)
With 3.5 mm hook, make 93 [107:121:135] ch.

1st row (RS): 1 dc into 2nd ch from hook, * 1 tr into next ch**, 1 dc into next ch, rep from * to end, ending last rep at **, turn. 92 [106:120:134] sts. Now work in patt as follows:

2nd row: 1 ch (does NOT count as st), 1 dc into tr at base of 1 ch, *1 tr into next dc **, 1 dc into next tr, rep from * to end, ending last rep at **, turn. This row forms patt.
Work in patt for another 4 [6:8:10] rows, ending with RS facing for next row.

Girl's version only
Next row (buttonhole row) (RS): Patt 2 sts, 1 ch, miss 1 st (to make first buttonhole of first pair – on next row, work appropriate st into this ch sp), patt 6 [8:10:12] sts, 1 ch, miss 1 st (to make second buttonhole of first pair – on next row, work appropriate st into this ch sp), patt to end, turn.

Boy's version only
Next row (buttonhole row) (RS): Patt to last 10 [12:14:16] sts, 1 ch, miss 1 st (to make first buttonhole of first pair – on next row, work appropriate st into this ch sp), patt 6 [8.10.12] sts, 1 ch, miss 1 st (to make second buttonhole of first pair – on next row, work appropriate st

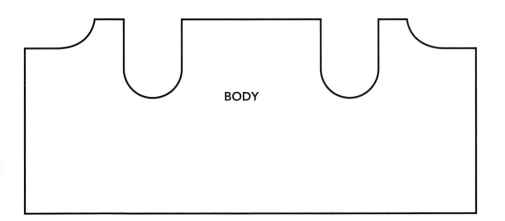

BODY

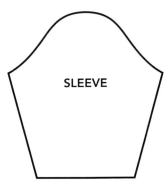

SLEEVE

into this ch sp), patt last 2 sts, turn.

Both versions
Patt a further 7 [9:9:11] rows, ending with RS facing for next row.
Rep the buttonhole row once more.
Cont straight until Body measures 13 [16:19:22] cm (5 [6¼:7½:8½] in), ending with RS facing for next row.

DIVIDE FOR ARMHOLES
Next row (RS): Patt first 24 [28:31:35] sts and turn, leaving rem sts unworked.
Work on this set of 24 [28:31:35] sts only for right front.
Keeping patt correct, dec 1 st at armhole edge of next 4 [5:6:7] rows. 20 [23:25:28] sts.
Cont straight until armhole measures 6 [7:7:8] cm (2¼ [2¾:2¾:3] in), ending with RS facing for next row.

SHAPE NECK
Keeping patt correct, dec 10 [12:13:15] sts at front opening edge of next row. 10 [11:12:13] sts.
Dec 1 st at neck edge of next 4 rows, then on foll 0 [0:1:1] alt row. 6 [7:7:8] sts.
Cont straight until armhole measures 10 [11:12:13] cm (4 [4¼:4¾:5] in), ending with RS facing for next row.

SHAPE SHOULDER
Fasten off.

SHAPE BACK
Return to last complete row worked, miss next 4 [4:6:6] sts, attach yarn to next st, patt 36 [42:46:52] sts and turn, leaving rem sts unworked.
Work on this set of 36 [42:46:52] sts only for back.
Keeping patt correct, dec 1 st at

each end of next 4 [5:6:7] rows. 28 [32:34:38] sts.
Cont straight until armhole measures 10 [11:12:13] cm (4 [4¼:4¾:5] in), ending with RS facing for next row.

SHAPE SHOULDER
Fasten off, placing markers at each side of centre 16 [18:20:22] sts to denote back neck.

SHAPE LEFT FRONT
Return to last complete row worked, miss next 4 [4:6:6] sts, attach yarn to next st, patt to end. 24 [28:31:35] sts.
Complete to match right front, reversing shapings.

Sleeves

With 3.5 mm hook, make 21 [23:25:27] ch.
Work first and 2nd rows as given for Body. 20 [22:24:26] sts.
Cont in patt, shaping sides by inc 1 st at each end of next and foll 5 [4:3:2] alt rows, then on 0 [2:4:6] foll 3rd rows. 32 [36:40:44] sts.
Cont straight until Sleeve measures 12 [15:19:23] cm (4¾ [6:7½:9] in), ending with RS facing for next row.

SHAPE TOP
Keeping patt correct, dec 2 [2:3:3] sts at each end of next row. 28 [32:34:38] sts.
Dec 1 st at each end of next 9 [11:11:13] rows, ending with RS facing for next row. 10 [10:12:12] sts.
Fasten off.

Making up

Join shoulder seams.

COLLAR
With 3.5 mm hook, make 39 [43:49:53] ch.
Work first and 2nd rows as given for Body. 38 [42:48:52] sts.
Cont in patt for 4 rows, ending with RS facing for next row.
Place markers at both ends of last row.
Dec 5 [6:7:7] sts at end of next 2 rows, then 6 [6:7:8] sts at end of next 2 rows. 16 [18:20:22] sts.
Fasten off.

Mark points along neck shaping 6 [7:8:9] sts in from front opening edges. Matching markers, sew shaped upper edge of Collar to neck edge between these points. Join sleeve seams. Matching top of sleeve seam to centre of sts missed at underarm and centre of last row of Sleeve to shoulder seam, sew Sleeves into armholes. Sew on buttons so that front opening edges overlap by 12 [14:16:18] sts.

STRIPED SWEATER

Bold stripes of colour add the interest to this classic sweater, worked in just trebles. The buttoned shoulder opening makes it easy to put on and take off too. Choose classic shades of blue as here, or soft and pretty pastels for a little girl.

MEASUREMENTS					
age (months)	0–3	3–6	6–12	12–18	
chest	41	46	51	56	cm
	16	18	20	22	in
actual chest	46	53	59	65	cm
	18	20¾	23¼	25½	in
length	21	25	29	33	cm
	8¼	9¾	11½	13	in
sleeve seam	12	15	19	23	cm
	4¾	6	7½	9	in

MATERIALS
- Rowan Cashsoft DK (50 g balls): 1 [2:2:2] balls in A (Navy 514), 1 [1:2:2] balls in B (Blue jacket 535), and 1 [1:2:2] balls in C (Cream 500)
- 3.5 mm crochet hook
- 2 buttons

ABBREVIATIONS
See page 9.

TENSION
19 stitches and 9½ rows to 10 cm (4 in) measured over treble fabric using 3.5 mm hook.
Change hook size if necessary to obtain this tension.

STITCH DIAGRAM

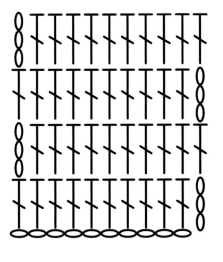

KEY

○ ch
🕈 tr

Shaping note

Decreases

Work all decreases at beg and ends of rows by working 2 sts together. Work dec at beg of row by working "3 ch (does NOT count as st – remember NOT to work into top of this 3 ch when working next row!), 1 tr into next st – 1 st decreased" and work dec at end of row by working "tr2tog over last 2 sts".

To decreases several sts at the end of a row, simply turn before the end of the row, leaving the "decreased" sts unworked. To decrease several sts at the beg of a row, ss along top of previous row, working a ss into each "decreased" st and then into what will be first st of next row. Work the "3 ch (counts as first tr)" and then complete the row.

Increases

Work all increases at beg and ends of rounds by working 2 sts into one st of previous round. Work inc at beg of round by working "3 ch (counts as first tr), 1 tr into st at base of 3 ch – 1 st increased" and work inc at end of round by working "2 tr into last st".

Stripe sequence

After first 3 rounds have been worked, work in stripes as follows:
4 rounds (or rows) using B.
2 rounds (or rows) using C.
4 rounds (or rows) using A.
2 rounds (or rows) using B.
4 rounds (or rows) using C.
2 rounds (or rows) using A.

These 18 rounds (or rows) form stripe sequence and are repeated as required.

Body

(worked in one piece to armholes)
With 3.5 mm hook and A, make 88 [100:112:124] ch and join with a ss to form a ring.
1st round (WS): 1 ch (does NOT count as st), 1 dc into each ch to end, ss to first dc, turn. 88 [100:112:124] sts.
2nd round: 1 ch (does NOT count as st), 1 dc into each dc to end, ss to first dc, turn.
Now work in tr fabric as follows:
3rd round (WS): 3 ch (counts as first tr), miss st at base of 3 ch, 1 tr into each st to end, ss to top of 3 ch at beg of round, turn.
This round forms tr fabric.
Joining in colours as required, now work in tr fabric in stripe sequence (see above and starting with 4 rounds using B) for another 8 [11:14:17] rounds, ending after 2 [1:2:1] rounds using A [B:C:A]. (A total of 11 [14:17:20] rounds completed from foundation ch edge.)

SHAPE BACK

Next row: Ss across first 3 sts of next "round" and into 4th st, 3 ch (counts as first tr), miss st at base of 3 ch, 1 tr into each of next 37 [43:49:55] tr and turn, leaving rem sts unworked.
Now working backwards and forwards in rows, not rounds, but keeping stripes correct, work on this set of 38 [44:50:56] sts only for back as follows:

Dec 1 st at each end of next 4 [5:6:7] rows. 30 [34:38:42] sts.
Work another 5 rows, ending after 2 [4:2:2] rows using A [B:A:B] and with RS facing for next row. Armhole should measure approx 10 [11:12:13] cm (4 [4¼:4¾:5] in.)

SHAPE SHOULDERS

Fasten off, placing markers at each side of centre 20 [22:24:26] sts to denote back neck, and at ends of last row to denote shoulder points.

LEFT BACK SHOULDER BUTTON BAND

With RS facing, miss first 25 [28:31:34] sts of next row, keeping stripe sequence correct attach appropriate yarn to next st, 1 ch (does NOT count as st), 1 dc into st at base of 1 ch, 1 dc into each of last 4 [5:6:7] sts, turn. 5 [6:7:8] sts.
Next row: 1 ch (does NOT count as st), 1 dc into each st to end.
Fasten off.

SHAPE FRONT

Return to last complete round worked, miss next 6 sts, attach appropriate yarn to next st, 3 ch (counts as first tr), miss st at base of 3 ch, 1 tr into each of next 37 [43:49:55] tr and turn, leaving rem sts unworked.
Dec 1 st at each end of next 4 [5:6:7] rows. 30 [34:38:42] sts.

SHAPE FRONT NECK

Next row (WS): 3 ch (counts as first tr), miss tr at base of 3 ch, 1 tr into each of next 7 [8:9:10] tr and turn, leaving rem sts unworked. 8 [9:10:11] sts.
Dec 1 st at neck edge of next 3 rows.

5 [6:7:8] sts.
Work 1 row, ending after 2 [4:2:2] rows using A [B:A:B] and with RS facing for next row.

SHAPE SHOULDER
Fasten off.

SHAPE SECOND SIDE OF NECK
Return to last complete row worked, miss next 14 [16:18:20] sts, attach appropriate yarn to next st, 3 ch (counts as first tr), miss tr at base of 3 ch, 1 tr into each of last 7 [8:9:10] tr, turn. 8 [9:10:11] sts. Dec 1 st at neck edge of next 3 rows. 5 [6:7:8] sts.

LEFT FRONT SHOULDER BUTTON-HOLE BAND
Using A [B:A:B] only, complete this side of neck as follows:
Next row (WS): 1 ch (does NOT count as st), 1 dc into each of first 2 [2:3:3] sts, 1 ch, miss 1 st (to make a buttonhole), 1 dc into each of last 2 [3:3:4] sts, turn.
Next row: 1 ch (does NOT count as st), 1 dc into each dc and ch sp to end. Fasten off.

Sleeves

With 3.5 mm hook and C, make 22 [24:26:28] ch and join with a ss to form a ring.
Work first and 2nd rounds as given for Body. 22 [24:26:28] sts.
Starting with 1 [0:1:2] further rounds using C and then 2 rounds using A, cont in tr fabric in stripe sequence as given for Body as follows:
Inc 1 st at each end of next 7 [7:5:3] rounds, then on foll 1 [2:5:8] alt

rounds. 38 [42:46:50] sts.
Work another 2 rounds, ending after 2 [1:2:1] rounds using A [B:C:A]. Sleeve should measure 12 [15:19:23] cm (4¾ [6:7½:9] in).

SHAPE TOP
Keeping stripes correct but now working backwards and forwards in rows, not rounds, dec 3 sts at each end of next row. 32 [36:40:44] sts.
Dec 1 st at each end of next 5 rows. 22 [26:30:34] sts.
Fasten off.

Making up

Join right shoulder seam. Arrange left front shoulder buttonhole band over left back shoulder button band so that top of buttonhole band matches top of last tr row of Back and sew together at armhole edge.

NECKBAND
With RS facing, 3.5 mm hook and C [A:B:A], attach yarn at top of neck edge of left front shoulder buttonhole border, 1 ch (does NOT count as st), work 1 row of dc evenly around entire neck edge, ending at top of last row of back neck shoulder button band, turn.
Missing dc as required to ensure Neckband lies flat, cont as follows:
Next row: 1 ch (does NOT count as st), 1 dc into each dc to last 3 dc, 1 ch, miss 1 dc (to make 2nd buttonhole), 1 dc into each of last 2 dc, turn.
Next row: 1 ch (does NOT count as st), 1 dc into each dc or ch sp to end. Fasten off.

Matching missed sts at underarm and centre of last row of Sleeve to shoulder seam, sew Sleeves into armholes. Sew on buttons to correspond with buttonholes.

RABBIT

This cute little rabbit is sure to charm any tiny tot. Simply made in double crochet, and using a pure wool yarn, his arms and legs are just the right size for baby's tiny hands to hold.

MEASUREMENT
Complete Rabbit measures approx 36 cm (14 in) from tips of ears to base of feet

MATERIALS
- Rowan Pure Wool DK (50 g balls):
  2 balls in A (Enamel 013) and 1 ball
  in B (Tea rose 025)
- 3.5 mm crochet hook
- Oddment of blue yarn for eyes
- Washable toy filling

ABBREVIATIONS
See page 9.

TENSION
19 stitches and 20 rows to 10 cm
(4 in) measured over double crochet
fabric using 3.5 mm hook.
Change hook size if necessary to
obtain this tension.

STITCH DIAGRAM

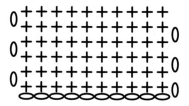

KEY   o ch
       + dc

Feet MAKE 2

With 3.5 mm hook and A, make 6 ch and fasten off (6 "V" shapes visible along length).
Attach A to 4th st from beginning of ch and cont as follows:
1st round (RS): 1 ch (does NOT count as st), 1 dc into ch at base of 1 ch, 1 dc into next ch, 2 dc into end ch, working back along other side of ch: 1 dc into each of next 4 ch, 2 dc into last ch, working back along rem section of first side of ch: 1 dc into each of next 2 ch, ss to first dc, turn. 12 sts.
2nd round: Using A 1 ch (does NOT count as st), 2 dc into first dc, 1 dc into next dc, 2 dc into each of next 2 dc, using B 1 dc into each of next 4 dc, using A 2 dc into each of next 2 dc, 1 dc into next dc, 2 dc into last dc, ss to first dc, turn. 18 sts.
3rd round: Using A 1 ch (does NOT count as st), 1 dc into each of first 4 dc, 2 dc into each of next 2 dc, using B 1 dc into each of next 6 dc, using A 2 dc into each of next 2 dc, 1 dc into each of last 4 dc, ss to first dc, turn. 22 sts.
4th round: Using A 1 ch (does NOT count as st), 1 dc into each of first 7 dc, using B 1 dc into each of next 8 dc, using A 1 dc into each of last 7 dc, ss to first dc, turn.
5th to 7th rounds: As 4th round.
8th round: Using A 1 ch (does NOT count as st), 1 dc into each of first 8 dc, using B 1 dc into each of next 6 dc, using A 1 dc into each of last 8 dc, ss to first dc, turn.
Now working in rows, not rounds, cont as follows:
9th row: Using A 1 ch (does NOT count as st), dc2tog over first 2 dc, 1 dc into each of next 2 dc, (dc2tog over next 2 dc) twice, using B 1 dc into each of next 6 dc, using A (dc2tog over next 2 dc) twice, 1 dc into each of next 2 dc, dc2tog over last 2 dc, turn. 16 sts.
10th row: Using A 1 ch (does NOT count as st), dc2tog over first 2 dc, 1 dc into each of next 4 dc, using B 1 dc into each of next 4 dc, using A 1 dc into each of next 4 dc, dc2tog over last 2 dc, turn. 14 sts.
11th row: Using A 1 ch (does NOT count as st), 1 dc into first dc, (dc2tog over next 2 dc) twice, 1 dc into next dc, using B 1 dc into each of next 2 dc, using A 1 dc into next dc, (dc2tog over next 2 dc) twice, 1 dc into last dc, turn. 10 sts.
Break off B and cont using A only.
Now working in rounds, not rows, cont as follows:
12th round: 1 ch (does NOT count as st), 1 dc into first dc, dc2tog over same st as already worked into and next dc, dc2tog over next 2 dc, 1 dc into each of next 2 dc, (dc2tog over next 2 dc) twice, 1 dc into same place as used for last "leg" of last dc2tog – this is last st of round, ss to first dc.
Fasten off.
Fold Foot flat with "hole" for Leg at centre and join seam across back of Foot.

Legs MAKE 2

With 3.5 mm hook and A, attach yarn to back of "hole" left in Foot for Leg and cont as follows:
1st round (RS): 1 ch (does NOT count as st), work 9 dc evenly around "hole", ss to first dc, turn. 9 sts.
2nd round: 1 ch (does NOT count as st), 1 dc into each dc to end, ss to first dc, turn.
Insert toy filling into Foot so Foot is quite firmly filled.
3rd to 20th rounds: As 2nd round.
Fasten off.
Insert toy filling into Leg so Leg is quite softly filled. Fold top of Leg flat so that Foot section extends forward from fold.

Body

BASE

With 3.5 mm hook and A, make 10 ch.
1st row: 1 dc into 2nd ch from hook, 1 dc into each ch to end, turn. 9 sts.
2nd row: 1 ch (does NOT count as st), 2 dc into first dc, 1 dc into each of next 7 dc, 2 dc into last dc, turn. 11 sts.
3rd row: 1 ch (does NOT count as st), 1 dc into each dc to end, turn.
4th row: As 3rd row.
5th row: 1 ch (does NOT count as st), dc2tog over first 2 dc, 1 dc into each dc to last 2 dc, dc2tog over last 2 dc, turn. 9 sts.
6th to 8th rows: As 5th row. 3 sts.
Fasten off.
Base is a triangular shape – foundation ch edge is front edge and last row is centre back edge.

BODY

With RS facing, 3.5 mm hook and A, attach yarn at centre of last row, 1 ch (does NOT count as st), work 9 dc evenly along one shaped edge to foundation ch edge, holding Legs against RS of Base, work 1 dc into each of first 4 foundation ch enclosing top folded edge of Leg in sts (make sure Foot points forward.), 1 dc into next foundation ch, now work 1 dc into each of last 4 foundation ch enclosing top folded edge of other Leg in sts, now work 9 dc evenly up other shaped edge of Base to point where yarn was rejoined, ss to first dc, turn. 27 sts.

1st round (WS): 1 ch (does NOT count as st), 2 dc into first dc, (1 dc into each of next 7 dc, 2 dc into each of next 2 dc) twice, 1 dc into each of next 7 dc, 2 dc into last dc, ss to first dc, turn. 33 sts.

2nd round: Using A 1 ch (does NOT count as st), 2 dc into first dc, 1 dc into each of next 9 dc, 2 dc into each of next 2 dc, 1 dc into next dc, using B 1 dc into each of next 7 dc, using A 1 dc into next dc, 2 dc into each of next 2 dc, 1 dc into each of next 9 dc, 2 dc into last dc, ss to first dc, turn. 39 sts.

3rd round: Using A 1 ch (does NOT count as st), 1 dc into each of first 15 dc, using B 1 dc into each of next 9 dc, using A 1 dc into each of last 15 dc, ss to first dc, turn.

4th to 6th rounds: As 3rd round.

7th round: Using A 1 ch (does NOT count as st), 1 dc into each of first 16 dc, using B 1 dc into each of next 7 dc, using A 1 dc into each of last 16 dc, ss to first dc, turn.

8th round: Using A 1 ch (does NOT count as st), dc2tog over first 2 dc, 1 dc into each of next 9 dc, (dc2tog over next 2 dc) twice, 1 dc into next dc, using B 1 dc into each of next 7 dc, using A 1 dc into next dc, (dc2tog over next 2 dc) twice, 1 dc into each of next 9 dc, dc2tog over last 2 dc, ss to first dc, turn. 33 sts.

9th round: Using A 1 ch (does NOT count as st), 1 dc into each of first 14 dc, using B 1 dc into each of next 5 dc, using A 1 dc into each of last 14 dc, ss to first dc, turn.

10th round: Using A 1 ch (does NOT count as st), dc2tog over first 2 dc, 1 dc into each of next 7 dc, (dc2tog over next 2 dc) twice, 1 dc into next dc, using B 1 dc into each of next 5 dc, using A 1 dc into next dc, (dc2tog over next 2 dc) twice, 1 dc into each of next 7 dc, dc2tog over last 2 dc, ss to first dc, turn. 27 sts.

11th round: Using A 1 ch (does NOT count as st), 1 dc into each of first 12 dc, using B 1 dc into each of next 3 dc, using A 1 dc into each of last 12 dc, ss to first dc, turn.

12th round: Using A 1 ch (does NOT count as st), dc2tog over first 2 dc, 1 dc into each of next 5 dc, (dc2tog over next 2 dc) twice, 1 dc into next dc, using B 1 dc into each of next 3 dc, using A 1 dc into next dc, (dc2tog over next 2 dc) twice, 1 dc into each of next 5 dc, dc2tog over last 2 dc, ss to first dc, turn. 21 sts. Break off B and cont using A only.

13th round: 1 ch (does NOT count as st), 1 dc into each dc to end, ss to first dc, turn.

14th round: 1 ch (does NOT count as st), dc2tog over first 2 dc, 1 dc into each of next 3 dc, (dc2tog over next 2 dc) twice, 1 dc into each of next 3 dc, (dc2tog over next 2 dc) twice, 1 dc into each of next 3 dc, dc2tog over last 2 dc, ss to first dc, turn. 15 sts.

15th round: As 13th round.
Fasten off.
Insert toy filling so that Body is firmly filled.

Head

With 3.5 mm hook and A, make 12 ch and join with a ss to form a ring.

1st round (RS): 1 ch (does NOT count as st), 1 dc into each ch to end, ss to first dc, turn. 12 sts.

2nd round: 1 ch (does NOT count as st), 1 dc into each of first 2 dc, 2 dc into each of next 2 dc, 1 dc into each of next 4 dc, 2 dc into each of next 2 dc, 1 dc into each of last 2 dc, ss to first dc, turn. 16 sts.

3rd round: 1 ch (does NOT count as st), 1 dc into each of first 3 dc, 2 dc into each of next 2 dc, 1 dc into each of next 6 dc, 2 dc into each of next 2 dc, 1 dc into each of last 3 dc, ss to first dc, turn. 20 sts.

4th round: 1 ch (does NOT count as st), 2 dc into first dc, 1 dc into each of next 3 dc, 2 dc into each of next 2 dc, 1 dc into each of next 8 dc, 2 dc into each of next 2 dc, 1 dc into each of next 3 dc, 2 dc into last dc, ss to first dc, turn. 26 sts.

5th round: 1 ch (does NOT count as st), 1 dc into each dc to end, ss to first dc, turn.

6th to 8th rounds: As 5th round.

9th round: 1 ch (does NOT count as st), 1 dc into each of first 5 dc, (dc2tog over next 2 dc) twice, 1 dc into each of next 8 dc, (dc2tog over next 2 dc) twice, 1 dc into each of last 5 dc, ss to first dc, turn. 22 sts.

10th round: As 5th round.

11th round: 1 ch (does NOT count as st), dc2tog over first 2 dc, 1 dc into each of next 2 dc, (dc2tog over next 2 dc) twice, 1 dc into each of next 6 dc, (dc2tog over next 2 dc) twice, 1 dc into each of next 2 dc, dc2tog over last 2 dc, ss to first dc, turn. 16 sts.

12th round: 1 ch (does NOT count as st), 1 dc into each of first 2 dc, (dc2tog over next 2 dc) twice, 1 dc into each of next 4 dc, (dc2tog over next 2 dc) twice, 1 dc into each of last 2 dc, ss to first dc, turn. 12 sts. Fasten off.

Fold Head flat with beg and end of rounds running up centre back and close top edge. Insert toy filling so Head is firmly filled, then sew foundation ch edge to top of Body, inserting a little more toy filling into neck section.

Arms MAKE 2

With 3.5 mm hook and A, make 2 ch.
1st round (RS): 6 dc into 2nd ch from hook, ss to first dc, turn. 6 sts.
2nd round: 1 ch (does NOT count as st), 2 dc into each of first 2 dc, 1 dc into next dc, 2 dc into each of next 2 dc, 1 dc into last dc, ss to first dc, turn. 10 sts.
3rd round: 1 ch (does NOT count as st), 1 dc into first dc, 2 dc into each of next 2 dc, 1 dc into each of next 3 dc, 2 dc into each of next 2 dc, 1 dc into each of last 2 dc, ss to first dc, turn. 14 sts.
4th round: 1 ch (does NOT count as st), 1 dc into each dc to end, ss to first dc, turn.
5th to 10th rounds: As 4th round.
11th round: 1 ch (does NOT count as st), 1 dc into first dc, (dc2tog over next 2 dc) twice, 1 dc into each of next 3 dc, (dc2tog over next 2 dc) twice, 1 dc into each of last 2 dc, ss to first dc, turn. 10 sts.
12th to 16th rounds: As 4th round.

Now working in rows, not rounds, cont as follows:

17th row: 1 ch (does NOT count as st), dc2tog over first 2 dc, 1 dc into each dc to last 2 dc, dc2tog over last 2 dc, turn. 8 sts.
18th and 19th rows: As 17th row. 4 sts.
20th row: 1 ch (does NOT count as st), (dc2tog over next 2 dc) twice. 2 sts.
Fasten off.

Insert toy filling into Arm so Arm is quite softly filled. Fold top of Arm flat so that shaped edges form a diagonal line. Using photograph as a positional guide, sew Arms to Body just back from chest patch.

Ears MAKE 2

With 3.5 mm hook and A, make 2 ch.
1st round (RS): 6 dc into 2nd ch from hook, ss to first dc, turn. 6 sts.
2nd round: Using A 1 ch (does NOT count as st), 2 dc into first dc, using B 1 dc into next dc, using A 2 dc into each of next 2 dc, 1 dc into next dc, 2 dc into last dc, ss to first dc, turn. 10 sts.
3rd round: Using A 1 ch (does NOT count as st), 1 dc into each of first 6 dc, using B 1 dc into each of next 3 dc, using A 1 dc into last dc, ss to first dc, turn.
4th round: Using A 1 ch (does NOT count as st), 2 dc into first dc, using B 1 dc into each of next 3 dc, using A 2 dc into each of next 2 dc, 1 dc into each of next 3 dc, 2 dc into last dc, ss to first dc, turn. 14 sts.
5th round: Using A 1 ch (does NOT count as st), 1 dc into each of first 8 dc, using B 1 dc into each of next

5 dc, using A 1 dc into last dc, ss to first dc, turn.
6th round: Using A 1 ch (does NOT count as st), 1 dc into first dc, using B 1 dc into each of next 5 dc, using A 1 dc into each of last 8 dc, ss to first dc, turn.
7th to 14th rounds: As 5th and 6th rounds 4 times.
15th round: Using A 1 ch (does NOT count as st), 1 dc into each of first 9 dc, using B 1 dc into each of next 3 dc, using A 1 dc into each of last 2 dc, ss to first dc, turn.
16th round: Using A 1 ch (does NOT count as st), dc2tog over first 2 dc, using B 1 dc into each of next 3 dc, using A dc2tog over next 2 dc, 1 dc into each of last 7 dc, ss to first dc, turn. 12 sts.
17th round: Using A 1 ch (does NOT count as st), dc2tog over first 2 dc, 1 dc into each of next 3 dc, dc2tog over next 2 dc, 1 dc into next dc, using B 1 dc into each of next 3 dc, using A 1 dc into last dc, ss to first dc, turn.
18th round: Using A 1 ch (does NOT count as st), 1 dc into first dc, using B 1 dc into each of next 3 dc, using A 1 dc into each of last 6 dc, ss to first dc, turn.
19th round: Using A 1 ch (does NOT count as st), 1 dc into each of first 6 dc, using B 1 dc into each of next 3 dc, using A 1 dc into last dc, ss to first dc, turn.
20th and 21st rounds: As 18th and 19th rounds.
22nd round: As 18th round.
Fasten off.

Press Ear flat, then make a pleat at base, with section in B inside pleat. Using photograph as a positional guide, sew Ears to top of Head.

Tail

With 3.5 mm hook and A, make 2 ch.

1st round (RS): 5 dc into 2nd ch from hook, ss to first dc, turn. 5 sts.

2nd round: 1 ch (does NOT count as st), 2 dc into each dc to end, ss to first dc, turn. 10 sts.

3rd round: 1 ch (does NOT count as st), (1 dc into next dc, 2 dc into next dc) 5 times, ss to first dc, turn. 15 sts.

4th round: 1 ch (does NOT count as st), 1 dc into each dc to end, ss to first dc, turn.

5th and 6th rounds: As 4th round.

7th round: 1 ch (does NOT count as st), (1 dc into next dc, dc2tog over next 2 dc) 5 times, ss to first dc. Fasten off.

Insert a little toy filling into Tail, then sew to back of Body just above Base.

Making up

Using photograph as a guide, embroider French knot eyes using oddment of blue yarn. Using B, embroider satin stitch triangle for nose, then back stitch lines below nose to form mouth.

HOODED JACKET

Keep your little one cosy in this stylish hooded jacket. Made in a simple textured stitch using a soft and thick cotton and microfibre yarn, the jacket is quick to crochet. And as the yarn is machine washable too, it is a pretty and practical choice.

MEASUREMENTS					
age (months)	0–3	3–6	6–12	12–18	
chest	41	46	51	56	cm
	16	18	20	22	in
actual chest	49	55	61	68	cm
	19¼	21½	24	26¾	in
length	23	27	31	35	cm
	9	10½	12¼	13¾	in
sleeve seam	13	16	20	26	cm
	5	6¼	7¾	10¼	in

MATERIALS
- 5 [5:6:6] x 50 g balls of Rowan All Seasons Cotton in Bleached 182
- 5 mm crochet hook
- 4 buttons

ABBREVIATIONS
- **V-st** – 1 dc, 1 ch and 1 dc
See also page 9.

TENSION
19 stitches and 14 rows to 10 cm (4 in) measured over pattern using 5 mm hook.
Change hook size if necessary to obtain this tension.

STITCH DIAGRAM

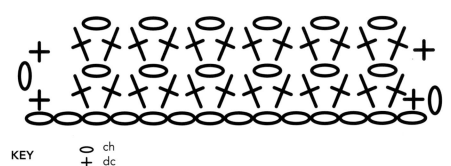

KEY
○ ch
+ dc

Body

(worked in one piece to armholes)
With 5 mm hook, make 102 [114:126:138] ch.

1st row (RS): 1 dc into 2nd ch from hook, miss 1 ch, *1 V-st into next ch**, miss 2 ch, rep from * to end, ending last rep at **, miss 1 ch, 1 dc into last ch, turn. 101 [113:125:137] sts, 33 [37:41:45] patt reps.
Now work in patt as follows:

2nd row: 1 ch (does NOT count as st), 1 dc into first dc, miss 1 dc, *1 V-st into next ch sp**, miss 2 dc, rep from * to end, ending last rep at **, miss 1 dc, 1 dc into last dc, turn.
This row forms patt.
Cont in patt until Body measures 12 [15:18:21] cm (4¾ [6:7:8¼] in), ending with WS facing for next row.

DIVIDE FOR ARMHOLES

Next row (WS): Patt until 7th [8th:9th:10th] V-st has been worked, miss 1 dc, 1 dc into next dc and turn, leaving rem sts unworked.

Work on this set of 23 [26:29:32] sts, 7 [8:9:10] patt reps only for left front. Cont straight until armhole measures 11 [12:13:14] cm (4¾ [4¾:5:5½] in), ending with RS facing for next row.

SHAPE SHOULDER

Fasten off, placing a marker 9 [11:13:15] sts in from armhole edge to denote inner edge of shoulder seam (14 [15:16:17] sts beyond marker at front opening edge).

SHAPE BACK

With WS facing, return to last complete row worked, miss next 10 sts, attach yarn to next dc, 1 ch (does NOT count as st), 1 dc into dc at base of 1 ch, miss 1 dc, 1 V-st into next ch sp, patt until 11 [13:15:17] V-sts in total have been worked, miss 1 dc, 1 dc into next dc and turn, leaving rem sts unworked.
Work on this set of 35 [41:47:53] sts, 11 [13:15:17] patt reps only for back. Cont straight until armhole measures 11 [12:13:14] cm (4¼ [4¾:5:5½] in), ending with RS facing for next row.

SHAPE SHOULDERS

Fasten off, placing markers at each side of centre 17 [19:21:23] sts to denote back neck.

SHAPE RIGHT FRONT

With WS facing, return to last complete row worked, miss next 10 sts, attach yarn to next dc, 1 ch (does NOT count as st), 1 dc into dc at base of 1 ch, miss 1 dc, 1 V-st into next ch sp, patt to end, turn. 23 [26:29:32] sts, 7 [8:9:10] patt reps. Complete to match left front. Do NOT fasten off at end of right front but slip working loop onto a safety pin and set aside this ball of yarn – it will be used later for Hood.

Sleeves

With 5 mm hook, make 24 [27:27:30] ch.
Work first and 2nd rows as given for Body. 23 [26:26:29] sts, 7 [8:8:9] patt reps.

3rd row: 1 ch (does NOT count as

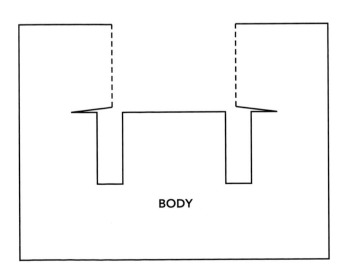

BODY

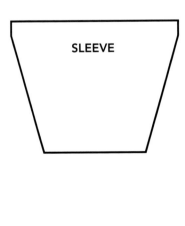

SLEEVE

st), 2 dc into first dc, miss 1 dc, 1 V-st into next ch sp, patt until V-st has been worked into last ch sp, miss 1 dc, 2 dc into last dc, turn.

4th row: 1 ch (does NOT count as st), 2 dc into first dc, 1 dc into next dc, miss 1 dc, 1 V-st into next ch sp, patt until V-st has been worked into last ch sp, miss 1 dc, 1 dc into next dc, 2 dc into last dc, turn.

5th row: 1 ch (does NOT count as st), 1 dc into first dc, 1 V-st into next dc, miss 2 dc, 1 V-st into next ch sp, patt until V-st has been worked into last ch sp, miss 2 dc, 1 V-st into next dc, 1 dc into last dc, turn.

29 [32:32:35] sts, 9 [10:10:11] patt reps.

Work 1 [3:3:5] rows.

Rep last 4 [6:6:8] rows 1 [1:2:2] times more, then 3rd to 5th rows again.

41 [44:50:53] sts, 13 [14:16:17] patt reps.

Cont straight until Sleeve measures 13 [16:20:26] cm (5 [6¼:7¾:10¼] in).

SHAPE TOP
Place markers at both ends of last row to denote top of sleeve seam.
Work another 3 rows.
Fasten off.

Making up

Join shoulder seams.

HOOD
Return to working loop left on safety pin at end of right front and slip this loop back onto 5 mm hook.
Working across sts of right front neck, back neck, then left front neck, cont as follows: 1 ch (does NOT count as st), 1 dc into first dc, miss

1 dc, 1 V-st into next ch sp, miss 2 dc, 1 V-st into next ch sp, (miss 1 st, 1 V-st into next st) 8 [9:10:11] times, 1 V-st into next ch sp (this is centre back neck ch sp), (1 V-st into next st, miss 1 st) 8 [9:10:11] times, 1 V-st into next ch sp, miss 2 dc, 1 V-st into next ch sp, miss 1 dc, 1 dc into last dc, turn. 65 [71:77:83] sts, 21 [23:25:27] patt reps.

Cont in patt until Hood measures 18 [19:21:22] cm (7 [7½:8¼:8½] in).
Fold Hood in half, with RS innermost, and join top seam of Hood by working a row of dc through sts of both edges.

Fasten off.

Join sleeve seams below markers. Matching sleeve markers to centre of sts missed at underarm and centre of last row of Sleeve to shoulder seam, sew Sleeves into armholes. Sew on buttons so that front opening edges overlap by 4 cm (1½ in) – use ch sps of V-sts as buttonholes, attach top button 6 cm (2¼ in) below first row of Hood, lowest button 5 cm (2 in) up from lower edge, and rem 2 buttons evenly spaced between.

WRAPOVER CARDIGAN

Quick and easy to make, this little cardigan is worked in a simple mesh of trebles and chains, with double crochet edgings. The merino wool, microfibre and cashmere blend yarn is ultra soft and machine washable too, making it really practical as well as pretty.

MEASUREMENTS					
age (months)	0–3	3–6	6–12	12–18	
chest	41	46	51	56	cm
	16	18	20	22	in
actual chest	44	49	55	60	cm
	17¼	19¼	21½	23½	in
length	17	21	25	29	cm
	6½	8¼	9¾	11½	in
sleeve seam	13	16	20	24	cm
	5	6¼	7¾	9½	in

MATERIALS
- 2 [3:3:4] x 50 g balls of Rowan Cashsoft DK
- 3.5 mm crochet hook

ABBREVIATIONS
- **beg dec** – dec 2 sts (1 ch sp) over first 3 sts as follows: 4 ch (does NOT count as st), miss 2 sts at end of previous row, 1 tr into next tr – 2 sts (1 ch sp) decreased
- **end dec** – dec 2 sts (1 ch sp) over last 3 sts of row as follows: yoh and insert hook into next tr, yoh and draw loop through, yoh and draw through 2 loops, (yoh) twice, miss 1 ch, insert hook into next st, yoh and draw loop through, (yoh and draw through 2 loops) twice, yoh and draw through all 3 loops on hook – 2 sts (1 ch sp) decreased
- **yoh** – yarn over hook.
See also page 9.

TENSION
22 sts and 10 rows to 10 cm (4 in) measured over pattern using 3.5 mm hook.
Change hook size if necessary to obtain this tension.

STITCH DIAGRAM

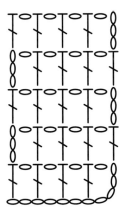

KEY
○ ch
┬ tr

Body

(worked in one piece to armholes)
With 3.5 mm hook, make 122 [140:154:168] ch.
1st row (RS): 1 dc into 2nd ch from hook, 1 dc into each ch to end, turn. 121 [139:153:167] sts.
2nd row: 4 ch (counts as first tr and 1 ch), miss first 2 dc, 1 tr into next dc, *1 ch, miss 1 dc, 1 tr into next dc, rep from * to end, turn. 60 [69:76:83] ch sps.
Now work in mesh patt as follows:
3rd row: 4 ch (counts as first tr and 1 ch), miss (tr at base of 4 ch and 1 ch), 1 tr into next tr, *1 ch, miss 1 ch, 1 tr into next tr, rep from * to end, working tr at end of last rep into 3rd of 4 ch at beg of previous row, turn.
This row forms mesh patt.

SHAPE FRONT SLOPES
Working all decreases as given in abbreviations, dec 2 sts at each end of next 4 [7:8:6] rows, then on 0 [0:1:3] foll alt rows. 105 [111:117:131] sts.
Work 0 [0:0:1] row. Body should measure 7 [10:13:16] cm (2¾ [4:5:6¼] in).

DIVIDE FOR ARMHOLES
Next row: Beg dec 1 [1:0:1] times, patt 21 [21:24:25] sts, end dec and turn, leaving rem sts unworked.
Work on this set of 23 [23:25:27] sts only for first front.
Dec 2 sts at armhole edge of next 1 [2:2:3] rows and at same time dec 2 sts at front slope edge on next [next:next:2nd] and foll 0 [1:0:0] row. 19 [15:19:19] sts.
Dec 2 sts at front slope edge only on next [2nd:next:next] and foll 3 [0:0:0] rows, then on foll 1 [2:3:3] alt rows. 9 [9:11:11] sts.
Work 2 rows. Armhole should measure 10 [11:12:13] cm (4 [4¼:4¾:5] in).

SHAPE SHOULDER
Fasten off.

SHAPE BACK
Return to last complete row worked, miss next 3 sts, attach yarn to next tr and cont as follows:
Next row: Beg dec over st where yarn was attached and next 2 sts, patt 39 [45:51:57] sts, end dec and turn, leaving rem sts unworked.
Work on this set of 41 [47:53:59] sts only for back.
Dec 2 sts at each end of next 1 [2:2:3] rows. 37 [39:45:47] sts.

Work 7 [7:8:8] rows.

SHAPE BACK NECK AND SHOULDER
Next row: Patt 8 [8:10:10] sts, end dec and fasten off.

Return to last complete row worked before shaping back neck, miss next 15 [17:19:21] sts, attach yarn to next tr and cont as follows:
Next row: Beg dec over st where yarn was attached and next 2 sts, patt to end and fasten off.

SHAPE SECOND FRONT
Return to last complete row worked before dividing for armholes, miss next 3 sts, attach yarn to next tr and cont as follows:
Next row: Beg dec over st where yarn was attached and next 2 sts, patt 21 [21:24:25] sts, end dec 1 [1:0:1] times, turn. 23 [23:25:27] sts.
Complete to match first front, reversing shapings.

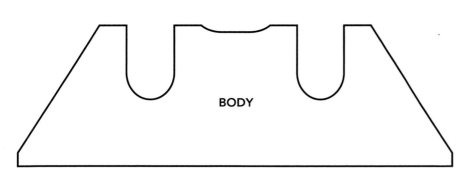

BODY

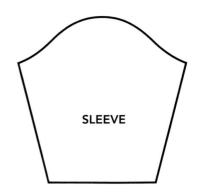

SLEEVE

5 [6¼:7¾:9½] in.)

SHAPE TOP
Next row: Ss across and into 3rd st, beg dec (4 sts in total decreased at this end of row), patt to last 5 sts, end dec and turn (4 sts in total decreased at this end of row). 35 [39:43:47] sts.
Dec 2 sts at each end of next 4 [5:6:7] rows. 19 sts.
Fasten off.

Making up

Join shoulder seams. Join sleeve seams. Insert sleeves into armholes, matching centre of last row of sleeve to shoulder seam and top of sleeve seam to centre of sts missed at underarm.

NECK AND FRONT EDGING AND TIES
With RS facing and using 3.5 mm hook, attach yarn at end of foundation ch edge of Body at base of right front opening edge, 1 ch (does NOT count as st), work in dc up row-end edges to start of front slope shaping, *118 [127:137:146] ch, 1 dc into 2nd ch from hook, 1 dc into each ch back to start of front slope shaping* – this forms first tie, work in dc up right front slope, around back neck, then down left front slope to start of front slope shaping, rep from * to * again to form second tie, then work in dc down remainder of left front opening edge to foundation ch edge. Fasten off.

Sleeves MAKE 2

With 3.5 mm hook, make 32 [32:36:36] ch.
Work 1st to 3rd rows as given for Body. 31 [31:35:35] sts, 15 [15:16:16] ch sps.
4th row: 5 ch (counts as first dtr and 1 ch), 1 tr into tr at base of 5 ch –

2 sts (1 ch sp) increased, patt to last st, (1 tr, 1 ch and 1 dtr) into last st – 2 sts (1 ch sp) increased, turn. 35 [35:37:37] sts.
Working all increases as set by last 2 rows, inc 2 sts at each end of 3rd [3rd:4th:4th] and 1 [2:2:3] foll 3rd [3rd:4th:4th] rows. 43 [47:51:55] sts.
Work 3 [3:4:4] rows. (Sleeve should measure 13 [16:20:24] cm,

CHEVRON TUNIC DRESS

Make your little one stand out in the crowd in this pretty little tunic dress! Bold stripes of colour are worked in a chevron pattern made up of trebles for the skirt and sleeves, with narrower stripes of double crochet making up the circular yoke.

MEASUREMENTS					
age (months)	0–3	3–6	6–12	12–18	
chest	41	46	51	56	cm
	16	18	20	22	in
actual size (at underarm)	44	51	58	64	cm
	17¼	20	22½	25	in
length (from upper edge)	26	32	38	45	cm
	10¼	12½	15	17¾	in
sleeve seam	13	16	21	27	cm
	5	6¼	8¼	10½	in

MATERIALS
- Rowan Pure Wool DK (50 g balls): 1 [2:2:2] balls in A (Dahlia 042), 1 [2:2:2] balls in B (Hyacinth 026), and 1 [2:2:2] balls in C (Tea rose 025)
- 3.5 mm and 4 mm crochet hooks
- 1 button

ABBREVIATIONS
- tr2tog – leaving last loop of each tr on hook work 1 tr into next st, miss next st, 1 tr into next st, yoh and draw through all 3 loops – 2 sts decreased.

See also page 9.

TENSION
18 stitches and 20 rows to 10 cm (4 in) measured over double crochet fabric using 4 mm hook.
Change hook size if necessary to obtain this tension.

STITCH DIAGRAM

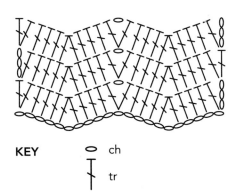

KEY

⬭   ch

†   tr

Ⱦ   tr2tog

Body

(worked in one piece to armholes)
With 4 mm hook and A, make
104 [124:144:164] ch.
1st row (RS): 1 tr into 4th ch from
hook, *1 tr into each of next 3 ch,
tr2tog over next 3 ch, 1 tr into each
of next 3 ch**, (1 tr, 1 ch and 1 tr)
into next ch, rep from * to end,
ending last rep at **, 2 tr into last ch,
turn. 10 [12:14:16] patt reps.
2nd row: 3 ch (counts as first tr), 1 tr
into tr at base of 3 ch, *1 tr into each
of next 3 tr, tr2tog over next 3 sts, 1 tr
into each of next 3 tr**, (1 tr, 1 ch and
1 tr) into next ch sp, rep from * to end,
ending last rep at **, 2 tr into top of
3 ch at beg of previous row, turn.
Last row forms chevron patt.
Joining in colours as required, now
work in chevron patt in stripes as
follows:
Using B, work 2 rows.
Using C, work 2 rows.
Using A, work 2 rows.
Last 6 rows form stripe sequence.
Work in chevron patt in stripe
sequence as set for another
5 [9:13:17] rows, ending after one
row using A [C:B:A].
Next row (WS): Using same colour
as for previous row: 1 ch (does NOT
count as st), 1 dc into first st, *miss
1 tr, 1 dc into next tr, 1 htr into next
tr, 1 tr into next tr, 1 dtr into next
tr2tog, 1 tr into next tr, 1 htr into
next tr, 1 dc into next tr, miss 1 tr**,
1 dc into next ch sp, rep from * to
end, ending last rep at **, 1 dc into
top of 3 ch at beg of previous row,
turn. 81 [97:113:129] sts.
Fasten off.

Sleeves

With 4 mm hook and C [A:A:A],
make 54 [54:64:64] ch.
Work first and 2nd rows as given for
Body. 5 [5:6:6] patt reps.
Working in chevron patt as now set
and stripe sequence as given for
Body, work another 7 [9:13:17] rows,
ending after one row using A [C:B:A].
Next row (WS): Using same colour
as for previous row: 1 ch (does NOT
count as st), 1 dc into first st, *miss
1 tr, 1 dc into next tr, 1 htr into next
tr, 1 tr into next tr, 1 dtr into next
tr2tog, 1 tr into next tr, 1 htr into
next tr, 1 dc into next tr, miss 1 tr**,
1 dc into next ch sp, rep from * to
end, ending last rep at **, 1 dc into
top of 3 ch at beg of previous row,
turn. 41 [41:49:49] sts.
Fasten off.

Yoke

Using 4 mm hook and B [A:C:B],
rejoin yarn to last st of last row of
Body and join Body and Sleeves as
follows:
1st row (RS): 1 ch (does NOT count
as st), 1 dc into first st, 1 dc into each
of next 8 [4:3:2] sts, dc2tog over
next 2 sts, (1 dc into each of next
0 [10:7:6] sts, dc2tog over next 2 dc)
0 [1:2:3] times, 1 dc into each of next
9 [5:4:3] sts, now work across
41 [41:49:49] sts of first Sleeve as
follows: 1 dc into each of first
4 [41:5:49] sts, (dc2tog over next
2 sts, 1 dc into each of next
8 [0:10:0] sts) 3 [0:3:0] times, (dc2tog
over next 2 sts) 1 [0:1:0] times, 1 dc
into each of last 5 [0:6:0] sts, now

work across next 41 [49:57:65] sts of
Body as follows: 1 dc into each of
next 5 [3:3:3] sts, dc2tog over next
2 sts, (1 dc into each of next
12 [8:6:5] sts, dc2tog over next 2 sts)
2 [4:6:8] times, 1 dc into each of next
6 [4:4:4] sts, now work across
41 [41:49:49] sts of second Sleeve as
follows: 1 dc into each of first
5 [41:6:49] sts, (dc2tog over next
2 sts, 1 dc into each of next
8 [0:10:0] sts) 3 [0:3:0] times, (dc2tog
over next 2 sts) 1 [0:1:0] times, 1 dc
into each of last 4 [0:5:0] sts, now
work across rem 20 [24:28:32] sts of
Body as follows: 1 dc into each of
first 9 [5:4:3] sts, dc2tog over next
2 sts, (1 dc into each of next
0 [10:7:6] sts, dc2tog over next 2 dc)
0 [1:2:3] times, 1 dc into each of next
9 [5:4:3] sts, turn.
150 [170:190:210] sts.
Keeping stripe sequence correct as
set by Body and Sleeves, cont as
follows:
2nd row: 1 ch (does NOT count as
st), 1 dc into each st to end, turn.
3rd row: 1 ch (does NOT count as
st), (1 dc into each of next 4 dc,
dc2tog over next 2 dc, 1 dc into
each of next 4 dc) 15 [17:19:21]
times, turn. 135 [153:171:189] sts.
4th and 5th rows: As 2nd row.
Change to 3.5 mm hook.

First size only
6th row: 1 ch (does NOT count as
st), (1 dc into each of next 3 dc,
dc2tog over next 2 dc, 1 dc into
each of next 4 dc) 15 times, turn.
120 sts.
7th and 8th rows: As 2nd row.
9th row: 1 ch (does NOT count as
st), (1 dc into each of next 3 dc,
dc2tog over next 2 dc, 1 dc into

each of next 3 dc) 15 times, turn.
105 sts.
10th row: As 2nd row.
11th row: 1 ch (does NOT count
as st), (1 dc into each of next 2 dc,
dc2tog over next 2 dc, 1 dc into each
of next 3 dc) 15 times, turn. 90 sts.
12th row: As 2nd row.
13th row: 1 ch (does NOT count
as st), (1 dc into each of next 2 dc,
dc2tog over next 2 dc, 1 dc into each
of next 2 dc) 15 times, turn. 75 sts.

2nd size only
6th row: 1 ch (does NOT count as
st), (1 dc into each of next 3 dc,
dc2tog over next 2 dc, 1 dc into
each of next 4 dc) 17 times, turn.
136 sts.
7th and 8th rows: As 2nd row.
9th row: 1 ch (does NOT count as
st), (1 dc into each of next 3 dc,
dc2tog over next 2 dc, 1 dc into
each of next 3 dc) 17 times, turn.
119 sts.
10th row: As 2nd row.
11th row: 1 ch (does NOT count as
st), (1 dc into each of next 16 dc,
dc2tog over next 2 dc, 1 dc into
each of next 3 dc) 5 times, 1 dc into
each of last 14 dc, turn. 114 sts.
12th row: 1 ch (does NOT count
as st), (1 dc into each of next 2 dc,
dc2tog over next 2 dc, 1 dc into
each of next 5 dc, dc2tog over next
2 dc, 1 dc into each of next 9 dc)
5 times, 1 dc into each of next 2
dc, dc2tog over next 2 dc, 1 dc into
each of next 5 dc, dc2tog over next
2 dc, 1 dc into each of last 3 dc,
turn. 102 sts.
13th row: 1 ch (does NOT count as
st), (1 dc into each of next 14 dc,
dc2tog over next 2 dc, 1 dc into
each of next 2 dc) 5 times, 1 dc into

each of last 12 dc, turn. 97 sts.
14th row: As 2nd row.
15th row: 1 ch (does NOT count
as st), (1 dc into each of next 2 dc,
dc2tog over next 2 dc, 1 dc into
each of next 4 dc, dc2tog over next
2 dc, 1 dc into each of next 3 dc,
dc2tog over next 2 dc, 1 dc into
each of next 2 dc) 5 times, 1 dc into
each of next 2 dc, dc2tog over next
2 dc, 1 dc into each of next 4 dc,
dc2tog over next 2 dc, 1 dc into
each of last 2 dc, turn. 80 sts.

3rd size only
6th row: 1 ch (does NOT count as
st), (1 dc into each of next 12 dc,
dc2tog over next 2 dc, 1 dc into
each of next 4 dc) 9 times, 1 dc into
each of last 9 dc, turn. 162 sts.
7th row: 1 ch (does NOT count as
st), (1 dc into each of next 3 dc,
dc2tog over next 2 dc, 1 dc into
each of next 12 dc) 9 times, 1 dc
into each of next 3 dc, dc2tog over
next 2 dc, 1 dc into each of last 4 dc,
turn. 152 sts.
8th row: As 2nd row.
9th row: 1 ch (does NOT count as
st), (1 dc into each of next 11 dc,
dc2tog over next 2 dc, 1 dc into
each of next 3 dc) 9 times, 1 dc into
each of last 8 dc, turn. 143 sts.
10th row: 1 ch (does NOT count
as st), (1 dc into each of next 3 dc,
dc2tog over next 2 dc, 1 dc into
each of next 10 dc) 9 times, 1 dc
into each of next 3 dc, dc2tog over
next 2 dc, 1 dc into each of last 3 dc,
turn. 133 sts.
11th row: As 2nd row.
12th row: 1 ch (does NOT count
as st), (1 dc into each of next 9 dc,
dc2tog over next 2 dc, 1 dc into
each of next 3 dc) 9 times, 1 dc into

each of last 7 dc, turn. 124 sts.
13th row: 1 ch (does NOT count
as st), (1 dc into each of next 2 dc,
dc2tog over next 2 dc, 1 dc into
each of next 9 dc) 9 times, 1 dc into
each of next 2 dc, dc2tog over next
2 dc, 1 dc into each of last 3 dc,
turn. 114 sts.
14th row: As 2nd row.
15th row: 1 ch (does NOT count
as st), (1 dc into each of next 8 dc,
dc2tog over next 2 dc, 1 dc into
each of next 2 dc) 9 times, 1 dc into
each of last 6 dc, turn. 105 sts.
16th row: 1 ch (does NOT count
as st), (1 dc into each of next 2 dc,
dc2tog over next 2 dc, 1 dc into
each of next 7 dc) 9 times, 1 dc into
each of next 2 dc, dc2tog over next
2 dc, 1 dc into each of last 2 dc,
turn. 95 sts.
17th row: 1 ch (does NOT count
as st), (1 dc into each of next 6 dc,
dc2tog over next 2 dc, 1 dc into
each of next 2 dc) 9 times, 1 dc into
each of last 5 dc, turn. 86 sts.

4th size only
6th row: 1 ch (does NOT count as
st), (1 dc into each of next 3 dc,
dc2tog over next 2 dc, 1 dc into
each of next 16 dc, dc2tog over next
2 dc, 1 dc into each of next 4 dc)
7 times, turn. 175 sts.
7th row: 1 ch (does NOT count as
st), (1 dc into each of next 11 dc,
dc2tog over next 2 dc, 1 dc into
each of next 12 dc) 7 times, turn.
168 sts.
8th row: As 2nd row.
9th row: 1 ch (does NOT count as
st), (1 dc into each of next 3 dc,
dc2tog over next 2 dc, 1 dc into
each of next 14 dc, dc2tog over next
2 dc, 1 dc into each of next 3 dc)

7 times, turn. 154 sts.

10th row: As 2nd row.

11th row: 1 ch (does NOT count as st), (1 dc into each of next 10 dc, dc2tog over next 2 dc, 1 dc into each of next 10 dc) 7 times, turn. 147 sts.

12th row: 1 ch (does NOT count as st), (1 dc into each of next 2 dc, dc2tog over next 2 dc, 1 dc into each of next 12 dc, dc2tog over next 2 dc, 1 dc into each of next 3 dc) 7 times, turn. 133 sts.

13th and 14th rows: As 2nd row.

15th row: 1 ch (does NOT count

as st), (1 dc into each of next 2 dc, dc2tog over next 2 dc, 1 dc into each of next 4 dc, dc2tog over next 2 dc, 1 dc into each of next 5 dc, dc2tog over next 2 dc, 1 dc into each of next 2 dc) 7 times, turn. 112 sts.

16th and 17th rows: As 2nd row.

18th row: 1 ch (does NOT count as st), (1 dc into next dc, dc2tog over next 2 dc, 1 dc into each of next 4 dc, dc2tog over next 2 dc, 1 dc into each of next 3 dc, dc2tog over next 2 dc, 1 dc into each of next 2 dc) 7 times, turn. 91 sts.

19th row: As 2nd row.

All sizes

Next row (WS): 1 ch (does NOT count as st), 1 dc into each st to end, 5 ch (to make button loop), ss to last dc.

Fasten off.

Making up

Join sleeve seams. Join centre back seam, leaving seam open for 6 cm (2¼ in) at neck edge. Sew on button.

PUPPY PRAM STRING

Keep your little treasures amused while out in the buggy by entertaining them with these cute little puppies. Easily made in just double crochet, their cute little ribbon bows match the ribbon they are suspended from. Why not make one on its own and use it to decorate a rattle or keyring?

MEASUREMENTS
Each Puppy stands approx 10 cm (4 in) tall, and measures approx 11 cm (4¼ in) from nose to tail.

MATERIALS
- 1 x 50 g ball of Rowan Pure Wool DK in each of cream (Enamel 013) and dark brown (Earth 018)
- 1 x 50 g ball of Rowan Wool Cotton in light brown (Mocha 965)
- 1 x 50 g ball of Rowan Kid Classic in beige (Bear 817)
- 3.5 mm crochet hook
- Washable toy filling
- 120 cm (47¼ in) of 1 cm (⅜ in) wide tartan ribbon
- 120 cm (47¼ in) of 2.5 cm (1 in) wide tartan ribbon

ABBREVIATIONS
See page 9.

TENSION
19 stitches and 20 rows to 10 cm (4 in) measured over double crochet fabric using 3.5 mm hook. Change hook size if necessary to obtain this tension.

STITCH DIAGRAM

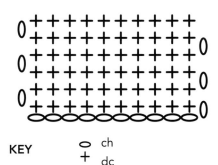

KEY

o ch

+ dc

Legs MAKE 4

With 3.5 mm hook and cream, make
3 ch.

1st round (RS): 2 dc into 2nd ch
from hook, 4 dc into last ch, working
back along other side of ch: 2 dc
into same ch as first 2 dc, ss to first
dc, turn. 8 sts.

2nd round: 1 ch (does NOT count as
st), 2 dc into first dc, 1 dc into each
of next 2 dc, 2 dc into each of next
2 dc, 1 dc into each of next 2 dc, 2
dc into last dc, ss to first dc, turn. 12
sts.

Break off cream and join in beige.

3rd round: 1 ch (does NOT count as
st), 1 dc into each dc to end, ss to
first dc, turn.

4th round: 1 ch (does NOT count
as st), 1 dc into each of first 4 dc,
(dc2tog over next 2 dc) twice, 1 dc
into each of last 4 dc, ss to first dc,
turn. 10 sts.

5th round: As 3rd round.

6th round: 1 ch (does NOT count as
st), dc2tog over first 2 dc, 1 dc into
each of next 6 dc, dc2tog over last
2 dc, ss to first dc, turn. 8 sts.

7th round: As 3rd round.

Fasten off.

Insert a tiny amount of toy filling and
fold top of Leg flat – start and ends
of rounds form back fold edge.

Tail

With 3.5 mm hook and light brown,

make 2 ch.

1st round (RS): 4 dc into 2nd ch
from hook, ss to first dc, turn. 4 sts.

2nd round: 1 ch (does NOT count as
st), 1 dc into each of dc to end, ss to
first dc, turn.

3rd round: As 2nd round.

Fasten off.

Fold Tail flat.

Body

BASE

With 3.5 mm hook and beige, make
5 ch.

1st row (RS): 1 dc into 2nd ch from
hook, 1 dc into each ch to end, turn.
4 sts.

2nd row: 1 ch (does NOT count as

st), 2 dc into first dc, 1 dc into each of next 2 dc, 2 dc into last dc, turn. 6 sts.

3rd row: 1 ch (does NOT count as st), 2 dc into first dc, 1 dc into each of next 4 dc, 2 dc into last dc, turn. 8 sts.

4th row: 1 ch (does NOT count as st), 1 dc into each dc to end, turn.

5th to 8th rows: As 4th row.

9th row: 1 ch (does NOT count as st), dc2tog over first 2 dc, 1 dc into each of next 4 dc, dc2tog over last 2 dc, turn. 6 sts.

10th row: As 4th row.

Fasten off.

Foundation ch edge of Base is back edge.

BODY

With RS facing, 3.5 mm hook and beige, attach yarn at centre of last row of Base and work around entire outer edge of Base as follows:

1st round: 1 ch (does NOT count as st), work 1 dc each of last 3 sts of "next" row of Base, then working 1 dc into each row-end edge and holding Legs against RS of Base, work 1 dc into each of first 4 row-end edges enclosing top folded edge of first Leg in sts (make sure Foot points toward front!), 1 dc into each of next 2 row-end edges, work 1 dc into each of next 4 row-end edges enclosing top folded edge of second Leg in sts, work 1 dc into each foundation ch of Base (4 sts), then working 1 dc into each row-end edge and holding Legs against RS of Base, work 1 dc into each of first 4 row-end edges enclosing top folded edge of third Leg in sts, 1 dc into each of next 2 row-end edges, work 1 dc into each of last 4 row-end edges enclosing top folded edge of fourth Leg in sts, then work 1 dc each of first 3 sts of "next" row of Base, ss to first dc, turn. 30 sts.

2nd round (WS): 1 ch (does NOT count as st), 2 dc into first dc, 1 dc into each of next 13 dc, 2 dc into each of next 2 dc, 1 dc into each of next 13 dc, 2 dc into last dc, ss to first dc, turn. 34 sts.

3rd round: 1 ch (does NOT count as st), 1 dc into each dc to end, ss to first dc, turn.

4th and 5th rounds: As 3rd round.

SHAPE OPENING FOR HEAD

Now working in rows, not rounds, cont as follows:

6th row: 1 ch (does NOT count as st), dc2tog over first 2 dc, 1 dc into each dc to last 2 dc, dc2tog over last 2 dc, turn.

7th row: As 6th row. 30 sts.

8th row: 1 ch (does NOT count as st), dc2tog over first 2 dc, 1 dc into each of next 11 dc, (dc2tog over next 2 dc) twice, 1 dc into each of next 11 dc, dc2tog over last 2 dc, turn. 26 sts.

9th row: 1 ch (does NOT count as st), dc2tog over first 2 dc, 1 dc into each of next 9 dc, (dc2tog over next 2 dc) twice, 1 dc into each of next 9 dc, dc2tog over last 2 dc, turn. 22 sts.

Fasten off. Fold Body in half and join top of last row to form top seam, enclosing end of Tail in seam near fold. Insert toy filling so Body is firmly filled.

Ears MAKE 2

With 3.5 mm hook and light brown, make 4 ch.

1st round (RS): 1 dc into 2nd ch from hook, 1 dc into each of next 2 ch, working back along other side of foundation ch: 1 dc into each of next 3 ch, ss to first dc, turn. 6 sts.

2nd round: 1 ch (does NOT count as st), 2 dc into first dc, 1 dc into next dc, 2 dc into each of next 2 dc, 1 dc into next dc, 2 dc into last dc, ss to first dc, turn. 10 sts.

3rd round: 1 ch (does NOT count as st), 1 dc into each dc to end, ss to first dc, turn.

4th and 5th rounds: As 3rd round.

6th round: 1 ch (does NOT count as st), dc2tog over first 2 dc, 1 dc into next dc, (dc2tog over next 2 dc) twice, 1 dc into next dc, dc2tog over last 2 dc, ss to first dc, turn. 6 sts.

7th round: As 3rd round.

8th round: 1 ch (does NOT count as st), 1 dc into each of first 2 dc, dc2tog over next 2 dc, 1 dc into each of last 2 dc, ss to first dc, turn. 5 sts.

9th round: As 3rd round.

Fasten off.

Fold Ear flat so that it forms a 6 shape – straighter edge is back edge.

Head

With 3.5 mm hook and beige, make 14 ch and join with a ss to form a ring.

1st round (RS): 1 ch (does NOT count as st), 1 dc into each ch to end, ss to first dc, turn. 14 sts.

2nd round: 1 ch (does NOT count as st), 2 dc into first dc, 1 dc into each of next 5 dc, 2 dc into each of next 2 dc, 1 dc into each of next 5 dc, 2 dc into last dc, ss to first dc, turn. 18 sts.

3rd round: 1 ch (does NOT count as st), 1 dc into each dc to end, ss to first dc, turn.

4th and 5th rounds: As 3rd round.

6th round: 1 ch (does NOT count as st), dc2tog over first 2 dc, 1 dc into each of next 5 dc, (dc2tog over next 2 dc) twice, 1 dc into each of next 5 dc, dc2tog over last 2 dc, ss to first dc, turn. 14 sts.

7th round: 1 ch (does NOT count as st), dc2tog over first 2 dc, 1 dc into each of next 3 dc, (dc2tog over next 2 dc) twice, 1 dc into each of next 3 dc, dc2tog over last 2 dc, ss to first dc, turn. 10 sts.

Fasten off.

Sew top seam of Head by joining top of last round and enclosing Ears in seam. Insert toy filling so Head is quite firmly filled. Sew foundation ch edge of Head to opening in Body, adding a little extra filling into neck section.

Muzzle

With 3.5 mm hook and cream, make 2 ch.

1st round (RS): 8 dc into 2nd ch from hook, ss to first dc, turn. 8 sts.

2nd round: 1 ch (does NOT count as st), 1 dc into first dc, 2 dc into each of next 2 dc, 1 dc into each of next 2 dc, 2 dc into each of next 2 dc, 1 dc into last dc, ss to first dc, turn. 12 sts.

3rd round: 1 ch (does NOT count as st), 1 dc into first dc, (2 dc into next dc, 1 dc into each of next 2 dc) 3 times, 2 dc into next dc, 1 dc into last dc, ss to first dc, turn.16 sts.

4th round: 1 ch (does NOT count as st), 1 dc into each dc to end, ss to first dc, turn.

5th to 7th rounds: As 4th round.

Fasten off.

Insert toy filling so Muzzle is quite firmly filled. Sew Muzzle to front of Head as in photograph. Catch stitch Ears to sides of Muzzle as in photograph.

Nose

With 3.5 mm hook and light brown, make 2 ch.

1st round (RS): 6 dc into 2nd ch from hook, ss to first dc, turn. 6 sts.

2nd round: 1 ch (does NOT count as st), (dc2tog over next 2 dc) 3 times, ss to first dc. 3 sts.

Fasten off.

Using photograph as a guide, sew Nose to Muzzle.

Making up

Using photograph as a guide and dark brown yarn, embroider French knot eyes and straight stitch mouth. Tie 30 cm (12 in) length of narrow ribbon in a bow around neck. Thread wider ribbon through centre top of body and tie in a knot.

Make four Basic Puppies – two puppies using colours as given, and two puppies using colours as follows: use beige instead of cream, light brown instead of beige, and dark brown instead of light brown. Embroider eyes and mouths using darkest shade used for each puppy. Tie a knot in wider ribbon approx 30 cm (12 in) from one end. Using photograph as a guide, thread ribbon through top of first puppy just behind its neck, and tie ribbon in a knot again to secure this puppy in place. Knot ribbon again approx 6 cm (2¼ in) from last puppy, thread on next puppy and knot ribbon again to secure this puppy in place. Continue in this way until all 4 puppies are knotted onto ribbon, then trim free end of ribbon to match first end.

For a simpler, quicker project, just make one puppy and tie to a length of wide ribbon – this can then be attached to a rattle or highchair.

ALL-IN-ONE

Keep your cherub cosy and warm in this practical all-in-one. Simply made in just double crochet, the tweedy yarn creates the colour interest. It fastens with a practical zipped opening and the doubled cuffs at the wrist and ankles will keep out the cold.

MEASUREMENTS					
age	0–3	3–6	6–12	12–18	months
chest	41	46	51	56	cm
	16	18	20	22	in
actual chest (at underarm)	49	56	62	69	cm
	19¼	22	24½	27	in
length (from shoulder to ankle)	47	51	57	63	cm
	18½	20	22½	24¾	in
sleeve seam	12	15	19	23	cm
	4¼	6	7½	9	in

MATERIALS
- 6 [6:7:8] x 50 g balls of Twilleys Freedom Spirit
- 3.5 mm and 4 mm crochet hooks
- Zip to fit front opening

ABBREVIATIONS
See page 9.

TENSION
18 stitches and 21 rows to 10 cm (4 in) measured over double crochet fabric using 4 mm hook.
Change hook size if necessary to obtain this tension.

STITCH DIAGRAM

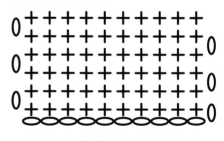

KEY   ○ ch   + dc

Body

FIRST LEG

With 3.5 mm hook, make 26 [30:34:38] ch and join with a ss to form a ring.

1st round (RS): 1 ch (does NOT count as st), 1 dc into each ch to end, ss to first dc, turn. 26 [30:34:38] sts.

2nd round: 1 ch (does NOT count as st), 1 dc into each dc to end, ss to first dc, turn.

Last round forms dc fabric worked in rounds.

Work in dc fabric for another 4 rounds.

Place marker at end of last round.

Work another 6 rounds.

Change to 4 mm hook.

13th round (RS): 1 ch (does NOT count as st), (1 dc into first dc) 0 [1:1:1] times, 2 dc into each of next 2 dc, (1 dc into next dc, 2 dc into each of next 2 dc) 8 [9:10:11] times, 1 dc into each of last 0 [0:1:2] dc, ss to first dc, turn. 44 [50:56:62] sts.

Cont in dc fabric until First Leg measures 10 [12:14:16] cm (4 [4¾:5½:6¼] in) from marked round, ending after a WS round.

Next round (RS): 1 ch (does NOT count as st), 2 dc into first dc, 1 dc into each dc to last dc, 2 dc into last dc, ss to first dc, turn. 46 [52:58:64] sts.

Work 1 round.

Next round: 1 ch (does NOT count as st), 2 dc into first dc, 1 dc into each dc to last dc, 2 dc into last dc, ss to first dc, turn. 48 [54:60:66] sts.

Rep last round 3 times more, ending after a WS round. 54 [60:66:72] sts.**

Break yarn.

SECOND LEG

Work as given for First Leg to **.

JOIN LEGS

Next round (RS): 1 ch (does NOT count as st), 1 dc into each dc of Second Leg, then 1 dc into each dc of First Leg, ss to first dc, turn. 108 [120:132:144] sts.

Work 3 [5:3:7] rounds.

Next round: 1 ch (does NOT count as st), 1 dc into each of first 25 [28:31:34] dc, (dc2tog over next 2 dc) twice, 1 dc into each of next 50 [56:62:68] dc, (dc2tog over next 2 dc) twice, 1 dc into each of last 25 [28:31:34] dc, ss to first dc, turn. 104 [116:128:140] sts.

Work 4 [6:9:9] rounds.

3rd and 4th sizes only

Next round: 1 ch (does NOT count as st), 1 dc into each of first [30:33] dc, (dc2tog over next 2 dc) twice, 1 dc into each of next [60:66] dc, (dc2tog over next 2 dc) twice, 1 dc into each of last [30:33] dc, ss to first dc, turn. [124:136] sts.

Work [1:0] rounds.

ALL SIZES

Next row: 1 ch (does NOT count as st), 1 dc into each dc to end, turn.

Last row forms dc fabric worked in rows.

Work in dc fabric for another 2 [0:7:8] rows.

Next row: 1 ch (does NOT count as st), 1 dc into each of first 24 [27:29:32] dc, (dc2tog over next 2 dc) twice, 1 dc into each of next 48 [54:58:64] dc, (dc2tog over next 2 dc) twice, 1 dc into each of last 24 [27:29:32] dc, turn. 100 [112:120:132] sts.

Work 7 [7:9:9] rows.

Next row: 1 ch (does NOT count as st), 1 dc into each of first 23 [26:28:31] dc, (dc2tog over next 2 dc) twice, 1 dc into each of next 46 [52:56:62] dc, (dc2tog over next 2 dc) twice, 1 dc into each of last 23 [26:28:31] dc, turn. 96 [108:116:128] sts.

Work 7 [7:9:9] rows.

Next row: 1 ch (does NOT count as st), 1 dc into each of first 22 [25:27:30] dc, (dc2tog over next 2 dc) twice, 1 dc into each of next 44 [50:54:60] dc, (dc2tog over next 2 dc) twice, 1 dc into each of last 22 [25:27:30] dc, turn. 92 [104:112:124] sts.

1st and 2nd sizes only

Work 7 rows.

Next row: 1 ch (does NOT count as st), 1 dc into each of first 21 [24] dc, (dc2tog over next 2 dc) twice, 1 dc into each of next 42 [48] dc, (dc2tog over next 2 dc) twice, 1 dc into each of last 21 [24] dc, turn. 88 [100] sts.

All sizes

Cont straight until work measures 24 [25:28:31] cm (9½ [9¾:11:12¼] in) from leg joining row, ending after a WS row.

SHAPE BACK

Slip working loop onto a safety pin and set aside ball of yarn in use.

With RS facing, miss first 25 [28:31:34] sts of next row, rejoin new ball of yarn to next st and cont as follows:

Next row: 1 ch (does NOT count as st), 1 dc into dc where yarn was rejoined, 1 dc into each of next 37 [43:49:55] sts and turn.

Work on this set of 38 [44:50:56] sts only for back.

Dec 1 st (by working dc2tog over edge 2 sts) at each end of next 3 rows, then on foll 2 [3:4:5] alt rows. 28 [32:36:40] sts.
Cont straight until armhole measures 9 [10:11:12] cm (3¼ [4:4¼:4¾] in), ending after a WS row.

SHAPE BACK NECK
Next row (RS): 1 ch (does NOT count as st), 1 dc into each of first 7 [8:9:10] dc and turn, leaving rem sts unworked.
Dec 1 st at beg of next row.
6 [7:8:9] sts.

SHAPE SHOULDER
Fasten off.

Return to last complete row worked before shaping back neck, miss next 14 [16:18:20] sts, rejoin yarn to next st and work as follows:
Next row (RS): 1 ch (does NOT count as st), 1 dc into dc where yarn was rejoined, 1 dc into each of last 6 [7:8:9] dc, turn.
Dec 1 st at end of next row.
6 [7:8:9] sts.

SHAPE SHOULDER
Fasten off.

SHAPE RIGHT FRONT
Return to st left on safety pin. Slip this st back onto hook and cont as follows:
Next row (RS): 1 ch (does NOT count as st), 1 dc into each of first 19 [22:25:28] dc and turn. (There should be 6 dc left unworked between last st of right front and first st of back.)
Dec 1 st at armhole edge of next 3 rows, then on foll 2 [3:4:5] alt rows.

14 [16:18:20] sts.
Cont straight until 8 [8:10:10] rows less have been worked than on back to shoulder fasten-off point, ending after a WS row.

SHAPE NECK
Next row (RS): Ss across and into 4th [5th:5th:6th] dc, 1 ch (does NOT count as st), 1 dc into same place as last ss – 3 [4:4:5] sts decreased, 1 dc into each dc to end, turn.
11 [12:14:15] sts.
Dec 1 st at neck edge of next 4 rows, then on foll 1 [1:2:2] alt rows.
6 [7:8:9] sts.
Work 1 row.

SHAPE SHOULDER
Fasten off.

SHAPE LEFT FRONT
Return to last complete row worked before shaping back, miss next 6 dc, re-join yarn to next dc, 1 ch (does NOT count as st), 1 dc into same place as where yarn was rejoined, 1 dc into each dc to end, turn.
19 [22:25:28] sts.
Dec 1 st at armhole edge of next 3 rows, then on foll 2 [3:4:5] alt rows.
14 [16:18:20] sts.
Cont straight until 8 [8:10:10] rows less have been worked than on back to shoulder fasten-off point, ending after a WS row.

SHAPE NECK
Next row (RS): 1 ch (does NOT count as st), 1 dc into each of first 11 [12:14:15] dc and turn, leaving rem sts unworked – 3 [4:4:5] sts decreased. 11 [12:14:15] sts.
Dec 1 st at neck edge of next 4 rows, then on foll 1 [1:2:2] alt rows.

6 [7:8:9] sts.
Work 1 row.

SHAPE SHOULDER
Fasten off.

Sleeves

With 3.50 mm hook, make 22 [24:26:28] ch and join with a ss to form a ring.
1st round (RS): 1 ch (does NOT count as st), 1 dc into each ch to end, ss to first dc, turn. 22 [24:26:28] sts.
Work in rounds of dc fabric for a further 5 rounds.
Place marker at end of last round.
Work a further 6 rounds.
Change to 4.00 mm hook.
13th round: 1 ch (does NOT count as st), 1 dc into each of first 4 [3:3:2] dc, 2 dc into each of next 2 dc, (1 dc into next dc, 2 dc into each of next 2 dc) 4 [5:6:7] times, 1 dc into each of last 4 [4:3:3] dc, ss to first dc, turn. 32 [36:40:44] sts.
Cont in dc fabric until Sleeve measures 12 [15:19:23] cm (4¾ [6:7½:9] in) from marked round, ending after a WS round and remembering to turn at end of last round.

SHAPE TOP
Working all shaping as given for Body and now working in rows, not rounds, dec 3 sts at each end of next row. 26 [30:34:38] sts.
Dec 1 st at each end of next 9 [11:13:15] rows. 8 sts.
Fasten off.

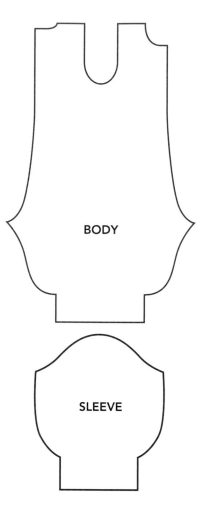

BODY

SLEEVE

dc down left side of neck to top of left front opening edge, turn. 38 [42:48:52] sts.
Work in rows of dc fabric for 13 rows, ending after a WS row.
Fasten off.

Sew zip into front opening, positioning top of zip teeth approx 4 rows up from first row of collar. Fold collar in half to inside and slip stitch in place. Fold first 6 rounds of legs and sleeves to inside and slip stitch in place.

Making up

Join shoulder seams. Sew sleeves into armholes.

COLLAR
With RS facing and using 3.5 mm hook, attach yarn at top of right front opening edge, 1 ch (does NOT count as st), work 11 [12:14:15] dc up right side of neck, 16 [18:20:22] dc across back neck, then 11 [12:14:15]

HOODED SWEATER

This cute little sweater is given extra impact by the use of a stunning hand-dyed yarn. The tweedy textures and bright colours of the yarn turn a simple stitch pattern into something really special. And, as the yarn is quite thick, it can be made really quickly too!

MEASUREMENTS					
age (months)	0–3	3–6	6–12	12–18	
chest	41	46	51	56	cm
	16	18	20	22	in
actual chest	48	55	62	68	cm
	19	21½	24½	26¾	in
length	23	27	31	35	cm
	9	10½	12¼	13¾	in
sleeve seam	13	16	20	26	cm
	5	6¼	7¾	10¼	in

MATERIALS
• 3 [3:3:4] x 100 g hanks of Colinette Prism in Neptune 139
• 5.5 mm crochet hook

ABBREVIATIONS
See page 9.

TENSION
12 stitches and 9 rows to 10 cm (4 in) measured over pattern using 5.5 mm hook.
Change hook size if necessary to obtain this tension.

STITCH DIAGRAM

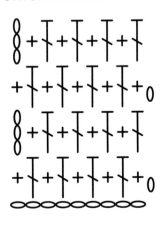

KEY
○ ch
+ dc
┬ tr

Back

With 5.5 mm hook, make
30 [34:38:42] ch.
Foundation row (RS): 1 dc into 2nd
ch from hook, *1 tr into next ch, 1 dc
into next ch, rep from * to end, turn.
29 [33:37:41] sts.
Now work in patt as follows:
1st row: 3 ch (counts as first tr), miss
dc at base of 3 ch, *1 dc into next tr,
1 tr into next dc, rep from * to end,
turn.
2nd row: 1 ch (does NOT count as
st), 1 dc into tr at base of 1 ch, *1 tr
into next dc, 1 dc into next tr, rep
from * to end, working dc at end of
last rep into top of 3 ch at beg of
previous row, turn.
Last 2 rows form patt.
Cont in patt until Back measures
approx 13 [16:19:22] cm
(5 [6¼:7½:8½] in), ending with RS
facing for next row.

SHAPE ARMHOLES

Next row (RS): Ss across and into
3rd st, 1 ch (does NOT count as st),
1 dc into tr at base of 1 ch – 2 sts
decreased, *1 tr into next dc, 1 dc
into next tr, rep from * to last 2 sts
and turn, leaving rem 2 sts unworked
– 2 sts decreased. 25 [29:33:37] sts.**
Cont straight until armhole measures
10 [11:12:13] cm (4 [4¼:4¾:5] in),
ending with RS facing for next row.

SHAPE SHOULDERS

Fasten off, placing markers at each
side of centre 11 [11:13:15] sts to
denote back neck.

Front

Work as given for Back to **.
Work 1 row, ending with RS facing
for next row.

DIVIDE FOR FRONT OPENING

Next row (RS): Patt 12 [14:16:18] sts
and turn, leaving rem sts unworked.
Cont in patt on these sts until Front
matches Back to fasten-off point.
Fasten off, placing marker 5 [5:6:7]
sts in from front opening edge to
denote front neck shoulder point.

With RS facing, return to last
complete row worked, miss next st,
attach yarn to next st, make turning
ch, patt to end, turn.
12 [14:16:18] sts.
Complete to match first side. Do
NOT fasten off but slip working loop
onto a safety pin and set aside this
ball of yarn – it will be used later
for Hood.

Sleeves

With 5.5 mm hook, make
18 [20:22:24] ch.
Work foundation row and first patt
row as given for Back. 17 [19:21:23]
sts.
Next row: 3 ch (counts as 1 tr),
1 dc into tr at base of 3 ch – 1 st
increased, *1 tr into next dc,
1 dc into next tr, rep from * to end,
working dc at end of last rep into
top of 3 ch at beg of previous row,
1 tr into same place as last dc – 1 st
increased, turn.
Working all increases in this way
(by working 2 sts into first and last
st of row) and keeping patt correct,
cont in patt, inc 1 st at each end of
2nd [3rd:3rd:4th] and every foll alt
[3rd:3rd:4th] row until there are
25 [27:31:33] sts.
Cont straight until Sleeve measures
13 [16:20:26] cm (5 [6¼:7¾:10¼] in),
ending with RS facing for next row.

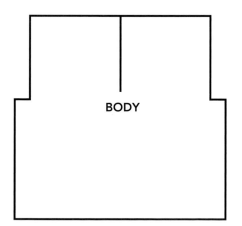

BODY

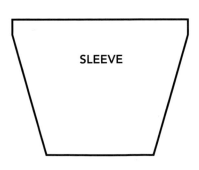

SLEEVE

SHAPE TOP

Place markers at both ends of last row to denote top of sleeve seam.
Work another 2 rows.
Fasten off.

Making up

Join shoulder seams.

HOOD

Return to working loop left on safety pin at top of right front opening edge and slip this loop back onto 5.5 mm hook.
With RS facing and working across 5 [5:6:7] sts of right front neck, 11 [11:13:15] sts of back neck, and then 5 [5:6:7] sts of left front neck, cont as follows: make turning ch and patt first 2 sts at right front neck edge, keeping patt correct as set by these 2 sts now work 2 sts into each of next 8 [8:10:12] sts, patt next st (this is centre back neck st), work 2 sts into each of next 8 [8:10:12] sts, then patt rem 2 sts at top of left front opening edge, turn.
37 [37:45:53] sts.
Cont in patt until Hood measures 13 [14:15:16] cm (5 [5½:6:6¼] in), ending with RS facing for next row.
Next row: Make turning ch and patt first 17 [17:21:25] sts, miss next st, 1 tr into next st (this is centre st of row), miss next st, patt to end, turn.
Next row: Make turning ch and patt to within 1 st of centre tr, miss next st, 1 tr into centre tr, miss next st, patt to end, turn.
Rep last row twice more.
29 [29:37:45] sts.
Fold Hood in half, with RS innermost, and join top seam of Hood by

working a row of dc through sts of both edges.
Fasten off.
Matching sleeve markers to top of side seam and centre of last row of Sleeve to shoulder seam, sew Sleeves into armholes. Join side and sleeve seams.

FRONT OPENING AND HOOD EDGING

With RS facing and using 5.5 mm hook, attach yarn at base of right front opening edge, 1 ch (does NOT count as st), work in dc evenly up right side of opening, then up right side of Hood, down left side of Hood, then down left front opening edge to base of opening, ss to first dc.
Fasten off.

GILET AND HAT

A fluffy yarn and a bobbly stitch pattern are combined to great effect for this cute little gilet and pull-on hat set! Made using a soft cashmere blend yarn worked together with a mohair and silk yarn, it's a little touch of cosy luxury for your angel.

MEASUREMENTS					
age (months)	0–3	3–6	6–12	12–18	
GILET					
chest	41	46	51	56	cm
	16	18	20	22	in
actual size	49	55	61	67	cm
	19¼	21½	24	26¼	in
length	22	25	29	34	cm
	8½	9¾	11¼	13¼	in
HAT					
width around head	31	36	40	44	cm
	12¼	14	15¾	17¼	in

GILET MATERIALS
- 2 [2:3:3] x 50 g balls of Rowan Cashsoft DK in M (Lake 543)
- 2 [3:3:4] x 25 g balls of Rowan Aura in C (Thunder 518)

HAT MATERIALS
- 1 [1:1:1] x 50 g ball of Rowan Cashsoft DK in M (Lake 543)
- 1 [1:1:1] x 25 g ball of Rowan Aura in C (Thunder 518)

GILET AND HAT
- 3.5 mm and 4.5 mm crochet hooks
- 5 buttons for Gilet

ABBREVIATIONS
See page 9.

TENSION
13½ stitches and 12 rows to 10 cm (4 in) measured over pattern using one strand of M and one strand of C together and 4.5 mm hook. Change hook size if necessary to obtain this tension.

Pattern and shaping note

This pattern is basically a dc fabric with tiny "bobbles" created on WS rows by working a taller dtr st. When shaping through patt, do NOT work these taller dtr sts on edge sts of rows as this may distort the work. Simply work them as a dc.

Decreases

To dec 1 st at beg of row, beg row with: "1 ch (does NOT count as st), dc2tog over first 2 sts – 1 st decreased".
To dec 1 st at end of row, patt to last 2 sts then work: "dc2tog over last 2 sts – 1 st decreased, turn".
To work a multiple dec at beg of row, ss across sts of previous row that are to be decreased and into what will become first st of new row, work 1 ch (does NOT count as st), and then 1 dc into st at base of 1 ch (this is same st as used for last ss). To work a multiple dec at the end of a row, simply turn the required number of sts before the end of the row, leaving the "decreased" sts unworked.

Increases

Work all increases at beg and ends of rows by working 2 sts into one st of previous row. Beg inc rows with: "1 ch (does NOT count as st), 2 dc into st at base of 1 ch – 1 st increased". End inc rows with: "2 dc into last st – 1 st increased, turn".

Gilet body

(worked in one piece to armholes)
With one strand of M and one strand of C held together and 4.5 mm hook, make 66 [74:82:90] ch.
1st row (RS): 1 dc into 2nd ch from hook, 1 dc into each ch to end, turn. 65 [73:81:89] sts.
Now work in patt as follows:
2nd row: 1 ch (does NOT count as st), 1 dc into first dc, *1 dtr into next dc, 1 dc into next dc, rep from * to end, turn.
3rd row: 1 ch (does NOT count as st), 1 dc into each st to end, turn.
4th row: 1 ch (does NOT count as st), 1 dc into each of first 2 dc, *1 dtr into next dc, 1 dc into next dc, rep from * to last st, 1 dc into last st, turn.
5th row: As 3rd row.
2nd to 5th rows form patt.
Work in patt for another 6 [8:12:16] rows, ending with WS facing for next row.

DIVIDE FOR ARMHOLES

Next row (WS): Patt first 13 [15:17:19] sts and turn, leaving rem sts unworked.
Work on this set of 13 [15:17:19] sts only for left front.

Keeping patt correct, dec 1 st at armhole edge of next 2 [3:3:4] rows, then on foll alt row. 10 [11:13:14] sts. Work 3 [4:2:3] rows, ending with WS facing for next row.

SHAPE NECK

Keeping patt correct, dec 2 [3:3:4] sts at front opening edge of next row. 8 [8:10:10] sts.
Dec 1 st at neck edge of next 2 rows, then on foll 1 [1:2:2] alt rows. 5 [5:6:6] sts.
Work 1 row, ending with WS facing for next row.

SHAPE SHOULDER

Fasten off.

SHAPE BACK

Return to last complete row worked before dividing for armholes, miss next 6 sts, attach yarn to next st, patt 27 [31:35:39] sts and turn, leaving rem sts unworked.
Work on this set of 27 [31:35:39] sts only for back.
Keeping patt correct, dec 1 st at each end of next 2 [3:3:4] rows, then on foll alt row. 21 [23:27:29] sts.
Work 7 [8:8:9] rows, ending with WS facing for next row.

SHAPE BACK NECK

Next row (WS): Patt first 6 [6:7:7] sts and turn, leaving rem sts unworked.
Keeping patt correct, dec 1 st at neck edge of next row, ending with WS facing for next row. 5 [5:6:6] sts.

SHAPE SHOULDER

Fasten off.

Return to last complete row worked before shaping back neck, miss next

STITCH DIAGRAM

KEY

- ○ ch
- + dc
- ⌿ dtr

9 [11:13:15] sts, attach yarn to next st, patt to end. 6 [6:7:7] sts. Keeping patt correct, dec 1 st at neck edge of next row, ending with WS facing for next row. 5 [5:6:6] sts.

SHAPE SHOULDER
Fasten off.

SHAPE RIGHT FRONT
Return to last complete row worked before dividing for armholes, miss next 6 sts, attach yarn to next st, patt to end. 13 [15:17:19] sts. Complete to match left front, reversing shapings.

Making up

Join shoulder seams.

FRONT, HEM AND NECK BORDER
With RS facing, 3.5 mm hook and M, attach yarn to foundation ch edge directly below left armhole, 1 ch (does NOT count as st), work one round of dc evenly across hem edge, up right front opening edge, around entire neck edge, down left front opening edge and across foundation ch edge, working 3 dc into corner points and ending with ss to first dc, turn.

Mark positions for 5 buttonholes along one front opening edge (right front for a girl, or left front for a boy) – position top buttonhole level with start of neck shaping, lowest buttonhole level with foundation ch edge of Body, and rem 3 buttonholes evenly spaced between.

Next round (WS): 1 ch (does NOT count as st), 1 dc into each dc to end, missing dc as required around neck edge to ensure Edging lies flat, working 3 dc into corner points, making buttonholes to correspond with positions marked by replacing (1 dc into each of next 2 dc) with (2 ch, miss 2 dc), and ending with ss to first dc, turn.

Next round: 1 ch (does NOT count as st), 1 dc into each dc to end, missing dc as required around neck edge to ensure Edging lies flat, working 3 dc into corner points, working 2 dc into each buttonhole ch sp, and ending with ss to first dc, do NOT turn.

Now work one round of crab st (dc

worked from left to right, instead of right to left) around entire outer edge, ending with ss to first dc. Fasten off.

ARMHOLE BORDERS

With RS facing, 3.5 mm hook and M, attach yarn at base of armhole, 1 ch (does NOT count as st), work one round of dc evenly around entire armhole edge, ending with ss to first dc, turn.

Next round (WS): 1 ch (does NOT count as st), 1 dc into each dc to end, ss to first dc, turn.

Next round: 1 ch (does NOT count as st), 1 dc into each dc to end, ss to first dc, do NOT turn.

Now work one round of crab st (dc worked from left to right, instead of right to left) around entire armhole edge, ending with ss to first dc. Fasten off.

Sew on buttons.

Hat

With one strand of M and one strand of C held together and 4.5 mm hook, make 42 [48:54:60] ch and join with a ss to form a ring.

1st round (RS): 1 ch (does NOT count as st), 1 dc into each ch to end, ss to first dc, turn. 42 [48:54:60] sts.
Now work in patt as follows:

2nd round: 1 ch (does NOT count as st), 1 dc into first dc, *1 dtr into next dc**, 1 dc into next dc, rep from * to end, ending last rep at **, ss to first dc, turn.

3rd round: 1 ch (does NOT count as st), 1 dc into each st to end, ss to first dc, turn.

4th round: 4 ch (counts as first dtr), miss st at base of 4 ch, *1 dc into next dc**, 1 dtr into next dc, rep from * to end, ending last rep at **, ss to top of 4 ch at beg of round, turn.

5th round: As 3rd round.
2nd to 5th rounds form patt.
Work in patt for another 3 [5:5:7] rounds, ending with RS facing for next round.

SHAPE CROWN

1st round (RS): 1 ch (does NOT count as st), (dc2tog over next 2 sts, 1 dc into each of next 4 sts) 7 [8:9:10] times, ss to first dc, turn. 35 [40:45:50] sts.
Keeping patt correct, work 1 round.

3rd round: 1 ch (does NOT count as st), (dc2tog over next 2 sts, 1 dc into each of next 3 sts) 7 [8:9:10] times, ss to first dc, turn. 28 [32:36:40] sts.

4th round: 1 ch (does NOT count as st), (patt 2 sts, dc2tog over next 2 sts) 7 [8:9:10] times, ss to first dc, turn. 21 [24:27:30] sts.

5th round: 1 ch (does NOT count as st), (dc2tog over next 2 sts, 1 dc into next st) 7 [8:9:10] times, ss to first dc, turn. 14 [16:18:20] sts.

6th round: 1 ch (does NOT count as st), (dc2tog over next 2 sts) 7 [8:9:10] times, ss to first dc, turn. 7 [8:9:10] sts.

7th round: 1 ch (does NOT count as st), (dc2tog over next 2 sts) 3 [4:4:5] times, (1 dc into last st) 1 [0:1:0] times, ss to first dc. 4 [4:5:5] sts. Fasten off. Run a gathering thread around top of last round of Hat, pull up tight and fasten off securely.

Making up

LOWER BORDER

With RS facing, 3.5 mm hook and M, attach yarn to foundation ch edge, 1 ch (does NOT count as st), work one round of dc evenly around entire foundation ch edge, ending with ss to first dc, turn.

Next round (WS): 1 ch (does NOT count as st), 1 dc into each dc to end, ss to first dc, turn.

Next round: 1 ch (does NOT count as st), 1 dc into each dc to end, ss to first dc, do NOT turn.

Now work one round of crab st (dc worked from left to right, instead of right to left) around entire lower edge, ending with ss to first dc. Fasten off.

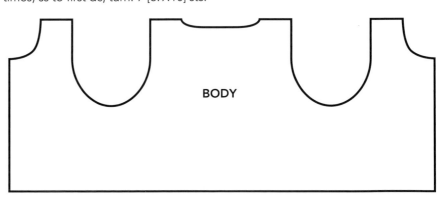

BODY

BOY AND GIRL DOLLS

These cute dolls are sure to delight any little one. Simply made in just double crochet using a DK weight yarn, their construction means there's very little sewing to do too! Their clothes are removable – so you could make them a whole wardrobe to wear.

MEASUREMENT
Complete Doll stands approx 30 cm (12 in) tall

MATERIALS
- Rowan Cashsoft Baby DK (50 g balls): 2 balls in pink (Sky pink 540) and 1 ball in cream (Cream 500)
- Rowan Cashsoft DK (50 g balls): 1 ball in each of navy (Navy 514), red (Poppy 512) and green (Lime 509)
- Rowan Pure Wool DK (50 g balls): 1 ball brown (Earth 018)
- 3.5 mm crochet hook
- Washable toy filling

ABBREVIATIONS
- loop 1 – insert hook into next st, form loop of yarn around first finger of left hand (for girl doll, draw out this loop to approx 10–12 cm/4–5 in, or for boy doll approx 2 cm/¾ in) and draw both strands of this looped yarn through st, yarn over hook and draw through all 3 loops on hook.

See also page 9.

TENSION
19 stitches and 20 rows to 10 cm (4 in) measured over double crochet fabric using 3.5 mm hook.
Change hook size if necessary to obtain this tension.

STITCH DIAGRAM

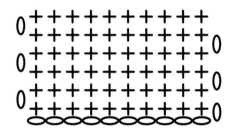

KEY   o ch
      + dc

Dolls legs *(make two)*

With 3.5 mm hook and pink, make 12 ch and join with a ss to form a ring.
1st round (RS): 1 ch (does NOT count as st), 1 dc into each ch to end, ss to first dc, turn. 12 sts.
2nd round: 1 ch (does NOT count as st), 1 dc into each dc to end, ss to first dc, turn.
3rd to 18th rounds: As 2nd round. Break off pink and join in cream.
19th to 21st rounds: As 2nd round. Break off cream and slip working loop onto a safety pin.
These 21 rounds form leg and ankle sock section. Now work foot as follows:

Girl doll

With WS facing, miss first 4 dc of next round, rejoin cream to next st, 1 ch (does NOT count as st), 1 dc into dc where yarn was rejoined, 1 dc into each of next 3 dc, turn. 4 sts.
Next row: 1 ch (does NOT count as st), 1 dc into each dc to end, turn.
Rep last row once more, ending with RS facing for next row.
Break off cream and join in navy.
Rep last row 3 times more, ending with WS facing for next row.
Fasten off.

Boy doll

With WS facing, miss first 4 dc of next round, rejoin brown to next st, 1 ch (does NOT count as st), 1 dc into dc where yarn was rejoined, 1 dc into each of next 3 dc, turn. 4 sts.
Next row: 1 ch (does NOT count as st), 1 dc into each dc to end, turn.
Rep last row 4 times more, ending with WS facing for next row.

Fasten off.

Both dolls

Return to working loop left on safety pin and slip this loop back onto hook. With WS facing and shoe colour (navy for Girl, or brown for Boy), work as follows: 1 ch (does NOT count as st), 1 dc into each of first 4 dc of last round worked before shaping foot, 5 dc evenly up row-end edge of top of foot section, 4 dc evenly across end of top of foot section, and 5 dc evenly down other row-end edge of top of foot section, then 1 dc into each of last 4 dc of last round, ss to first dc, turn. 22 sts.
Next round: 1 ch (does NOT count as st), 1 dc into each dc to end, ss to first dc, turn.
Rep last round twice more, ending with WS facing for next round.
Next round (WS): 1 ch (does NOT count as st), (1 dc into next dc, dc2tog over next 2 dc, 1 dc into each of next 5 dc, dc2tog over next 2 dc, 1 dc into next dc) twice, ss to first dc, turn. 18 sts.
Next round: 1 ch (does NOT count as st), (dc2tog over next 2 dc, 1 dc into each of next 5 dc, dc2tog over next 2 dc) twice, ss to first dc, turn. 14 sts.
Fasten off.

Fold foot section in half and join top of last round to form seam along base of foot. Insert toy filling so foot and leg are quite firmly filled. Fold top of leg flat, with start and ends of rounds at centre back.

Arms MAKE 2

THUMB

With 3.5 mm hook and pink, make 3 ch.
1st round (RS): 1 dc into 2nd ch from hook, 2 dc into next ch, working back along other side of ch: 1 dc into next ch (this is same ch as used for first dc), ss to first dc. 4 sts.
Fasten off.

HAND

With 3.5 mm hook and pink, make 4 ch.
1st round (RS): 1 dc into 2nd ch from hook, 1 dc into next ch, 2 dc into last ch, working back along other side of ch: 1 dc into each of next 2 ch (2nd of these is same ch as used for first dc), ss to first dc, turn. 6 sts.
2nd round: 1 ch (does NOT count as st), 2 dc into first dc, 1 dc into next dc, 2 dc into each of next 2 dc, 1 dc into next dc, 2 dc into last dc, ss to first dc, turn. 10 sts.
3rd round: 1 ch (does NOT count as st), 2 dc into first dc, 1 dc into each of next 3 dc, 2 dc into each of next 2 dc, 1 dc into each of next 3 dc, 2 dc into last dc, ss to first dc, turn. 14 sts.
4th round: 1 ch (does NOT count as st), 1 dc into each dc to end, ss to first dc, turn.
5th round: As 4th round.

JOIN THUMB TO HAND

6th round (WS): 1 ch (does NOT count as st), 1 dc into each of first 7 sts of Hand, 1 dc into each of next 4 dc of Thumb, 1 dc into each of last 7 sts of Hand, ss to first dc, turn.

18 sts.

Note: Where Thumb joins Hand, small hole is formed. It will be much easier to sew this hole closed now!

7th round: As 4th round.

8th round: 1 ch (does NOT count as st), 1 dc into each of first 7 dc, (dc2tog over next 2 dc) twice, 1 dc into each of last 7 dc, ss to first dc, turn. 16 sts.

9th round: 1 ch (does NOT count as st), 1 dc into each of first 6 dc, (dc2tog over next 2 dc) twice, 1 dc into each of last 6 dc, ss to first dc, turn. 14 sts.

10th round: 1 ch (does NOT count as st), dc2tog over first 2 dc, 1 dc into each of next 3 dc, (dc2tog over next 2 dc) twice, 1 dc into each of next 3 dc, dc2tog over last 2 dc, ss to first dc, turn. 10 sts.

11th to 20th rounds: As 4th round. Fasten off.

Insert toy filling so hand and arm are fairly firmly filled.

Body

BASE
With 3.5 mm hook and cream, make 14 ch.

1st row (RS): 1 dc into 2nd ch from hook, 1 dc into each ch to end, turn. 13 sts.

2nd row: 1 ch (does NOT count as st), 1 dc into each dc to end, turn.

3rd row: 1 ch (does NOT count as st), dc2tog over first 2 dc, 1 dc into each dc to last 2 dc, dc2tog over last 2 dc, turn. 11 sts.

4th to 6th rows: As 3rd row. 5 sts. Fasten off.

Base is a triangular shape – foundation ch edge is front edge and last row is centre back edge.

Body

With RS facing, 3.50 mm hook and cream, attach yarn at centre of last row and work around Base as follows:

1st round (RS): 1 ch (does NOT count as st), work 9 dc evenly along first shaped edge to foundation ch edge, holding Legs against RS of Base, work 1 dc into each of first 6 foundation ch enclosing top folded edge of Leg in sts (make sure Foot points forward.), 1 dc into next foundation ch, now work 1 dc into each of last 6 foundation ch enclosing top folded edge of other Leg in sts, now work 9 dc evenly along other shaped edge of Base to point where yarn was rejoined, ss to first dc, turn. 31 sts.

2nd round: 1 ch (does NOT count as st), 1 dc into each dc to end, ss to first dc, turn.

3rd and 4th rounds: As 2nd round.

5th round: 1 ch (does NOT count as st), 1 dc into each of first 7 dc, dc2tog over next 2 dc, 1 dc into each of next 13 dc, dc2tog over next 2 dc, 1 dc into each of last 7 dc, ss to first dc, turn. 29 sts.

6th round: 1 ch (does NOT count as st), dc2tog over first 2 dc, 1 dc into each of next 6 dc, dc2tog over next 2 dc, 1 dc into each of next 9 dc, dc2tog over next 2 dc, 1 dc into each of next 6 dc, dc2tog over last 2 dc, ss to first dc, turn. 25 sts.

7th round: As 2nd round.

8th round: 1 ch (does NOT count as st), 1 dc into each of first 5 dc, dc2tog over next 2 dc, 1 dc into each of next 11 dc, dc2tog over next 2 dc, 1 dc into each of last 5 dc, ss to first dc, turn. 23 sts.
Break off cream and join in pink.

9th round: 1 ch (does NOT count as st), dc2tog over first 2 dc, 1 dc into each of next 4 dc, dc2tog over next 2 dc, 1 dc into each of next 7 dc, dc2tog over next 2 dc, 1 dc into each of next 4 dc, dc2tog over last 2 dc, ss to first dc, turn. 19 sts.

10th round: As 2nd round.

11th round: 1 ch (does NOT count as st), 1 dc into each of first 3 dc, dc2tog over next 2 dc, 1 dc into each of next 9 dc, dc2tog over next 2 dc, 1 dc into each of last 3 dc, ss to first dc, turn. 17 sts.

12th round: 1 ch (does NOT count as st), dc2tog over first 2 dc, 1 dc into each of next 2 dc, dc2tog over next 2 dc, 1 dc into each of next 5 dc, dc2tog over next 2 dc, 1 dc into each of next 2 dc, dc2tog over last 2 dc, ss to first dc, turn. 13 sts.

JOIN ARMS TO BODY
13th round: 1 ch (does NOT count as st), 1 dc into each of first 3 dc of Body, 1 dc into each of next 10 dc of first Arm, 1 dc into each of next 7 dc of Body, 1 dc into each of next 10 dc of second Arm, 1 dc into each of last 3 dc of Body, ss to first dc, turn. 33 sts.

Note: Where Arms join Body, small holes are formed at underarm. It will be much easier to sew these holes closed now!

14th round: 1 ch (does NOT count as st), 1 dc into each of first 3 dc, dc2tog over next 2 dc, 1 dc into each of next 6 dc, dc2tog over next 2 dc, 1 dc into each of next 7 dc, dc2tog over next 2 dc, 1 dc into each of next 6 dc, dc2tog over next 2 dc, 1 dc into each of last 3 dc, ss to first dc, turn. 29 sts.

15th round: 1 ch (does NOT count as st), 1 dc into each of first 3 dc, dc2tog over next 2 dc, 1 dc into each of next 4 dc, dc2tog over next 2 dc, 1 dc into each of next 7 dc, dc2tog over next 2 dc, 1 dc into each of next 4 dc, dc2tog over next 2 dc, 1 dc into each of last 3 dc, ss to first dc, turn. 25 sts.

Insert toy filling so that lower section of Body is firmly filled.

16th round: 1 ch (does NOT count as st), 1 dc into each of first 3 dc, dc2tog over next 2 dc, 1 dc into each of next 2 dc, dc2tog over next 2 dc, 1 dc into each of next 7 dc, dc2tog over next 2 dc, 1 dc into each of next 2 dc, dc2tog over next 2 dc, 1 dc into each of last 3 dc, ss to first dc, turn. 21 sts.

17th round: 1 ch (does NOT count as st), 1 dc into each of first 3 dc, (dc2tog over next 2 dc) twice, 1 dc into each of next 7 dc, (dc2tog over next 2 dc) twice, 1 dc into each of last 3 dc, ss to first dc, turn. 17 sts.

18th round: 1 ch (does NOT count as st), 1 dc into first dc, (dc2tog over next 2 dc) 3 times, 1 dc into each of next 3 dc, (dc2tog over next 2 dc) 3 times, 1 dc into last dc, ss to first dc, turn. 11 sts.

19th round: As 2nd round.

Fasten off.

Insert toy filling so that upper section of Body and Arms are firmly filled.

Head

With 3.5 mm hook and pink, make 11 ch and fasten off. (11 'v' shapes visible along length of ch.)

1st round (RS): attach yarn to centre ch, 1 ch (does NOT count as st), 1 dc into ch where yarn was rejoined, 1 dc into each of next 4 ch, 2 dc into last ch, now working back along other side of foundation ch: 1 dc into same ch as last 2 dc, 1 dc into each of next 10 ch (last of these dc is worked into last ch), now working back along rem edge of foundation ch: 2 dc into same place as last dc, 1 dc into each of next 4 ch, 1 dc into same ch as dc at beg of round, ss to first dc, turn. 25 sts.

2nd round: 1 ch (does NOT count as st), 1 dc into each of first 6 dc, 2 dc into each of next 2 dc, 1 dc into each of next 9 dc, 2 dc into each of next 2 dc, 1 dc into each of last 6 dc, ss to first dc, turn. 29 sts.

Now working in rows, not rounds, cont as follows:

3rd row: 1 ch (does NOT count as st), dc2tog over first 2 dc, 1 dc into each of next 5 dc, 2 dc into each of next 2 dc, 1 dc into each of next 11 dc, 2 dc into each of next 2 dc, 1 dc into each of next 5 dc, dc2tog over next 2 dc, turn. 31 sts.

4th row: 1 ch (does NOT count as st), dc2tog over first 2 dc, 1 dc into each of next 5 dc, 2 dc into each of next 2 dc, 1 dc into each of next 13 dc, 2 dc into each of next 2 dc, 1 dc into each of next 5 dc, dc2tog over next 2 dc, turn. 33 sts.

5th row: 1 ch (does NOT count as st), 1 dc into each dc to end, turn.

6th row: 1 ch (does NOT count as st), 1 dc into each of first 7 dc, 2 dc into next dc, 1 dc into each of next 17 dc, 2 dc into next dc, 1 dc into each of last 7 dc, turn. 35 sts.

7th row: As 5th row.

Now working in rounds, not rows, cont as follows:

8th round: 1 ch (does NOT count as st), 2 dc into first dc, 1 dc into each dc to last dc, 2 dc into last dc, ss to first dc, turn. 37 sts.

9th round: 1 ch (does NOT count as st), 1 dc into each dc to end, ss to first dc, turn.

10th round: 1 ch (does NOT count as st), dc2tog over first 2 dc, 1 dc into each dc to last 2 dc, dc2tog over last 2 dc, ss to first dc, turn. 35 sts.

Fasten off.

Miss first 9 sts of next round, rejoin yarn to next dc and complete front of Head as follows:

11th row (RS): 1 ch (does NOT count as st), dc2tog over dc where yarn was rejoined and next dc, 1 dc into each of next 13 dc, dc2tog over next 2 dc and turn, leaving rem 9 sts unworked. 15 sts.

12th row: As 5th row.

13th row: 1 ch (does NOT count as st), dc2tog over first 2 dc, 1 dc into each dc to last 2 dc, dc2tog over last 2 dc, turn. 13 sts.

14th to 16th rows: As 13th row. 7 sts.

Fasten off.

Hair

With 3.5 mm hook and hair colour (cream for girl doll, or brown for boy doll), make 2 ch.

1st round (RS): 6 dc into 2nd ch from hook, ss to first dc, turn. 6 sts.

2nd round: 1 ch (does NOT count

as st), (loop 1) twice into each dc to end, ss to first st, turn. 12 sts.

3rd round: 1 ch (does NOT count as st), (2 dc into next st, 1 dc into next st) 6 times, ss to first dc, turn. 18 sts.

4th round: 1 ch (does NOT count as st), loop 1 into each dc to end, ss to first st, turn.

5th round: 1 ch (does NOT count as st), (2 dc into next st, 1 dc into next st) 9 times, ss to first dc, turn. 27 sts.

6th round: As 4th round.

7th round: 1 ch (does NOT count as st), 1 dc into first st, (2 dc into next st, 1 dc into next st) 13 times, ss to first dc, turn. 40 sts.

8th round: As 4th round.

9th round: 1 ch (does NOT count as st), (2 dc into next st, 1 dc into next st) 20 times, ss to first dc, turn. 60 sts.

10th round: As 4th round.
Fasten off.

Sew outer edge of Hair section to top of Head. Insert toy filling so Head is firmly filled, then sew neck opening of Head to top of Body, inserting a little more toy filling into neck section.

Making up

Using photograph as a guide, embroider French knot eyes using navy and french knot mouth using red. Carefully snip each 'loop 1' of hair section to create shaggy hair-like effect.

For girl doll, cut a double length of navy yarn and thread through foot and tie ends in a bow on top of foot as in photograph.

GIRL'S HAIR BOW

With 3.5 mm hook and red, make 18 ch and join with a ss to form a ring.

1st round (RS): 1 ch (does NOT count as st), 1 dc into each of first 2 ch, 1 tr into each of next 6 ch, 1 dc into each of next 3 ch, 1 tr into each of next 6 ch, 1 dc into last ch, ss to first dc, do NOT turn. 18 sts.

2nd round: Miss st at base of ss closing last round, 1 ss into next dc, 1 tr into each of next 6 tr, 1 ss into each of next 3 dc, 1 tr into each of next 6 tr, 1 ss into last dc.

Fasten off, leaving a long end.

Wrap this long end around centre of bow several times and secure end. Attach bow to top of head as in photograph.

Boy's shorts

FIRST LEG: With 3.5 mm hook and navy, make 21 ch and join with a ss to form a ring.

1st round (RS): 1 ch (does NOT count as st), 1 dc into each ch to end, ss to first dc, turn. 21 sts.

2nd round: 1 ch (does NOT count as st), 1 dc into each dc to end, ss to first dc, turn.

3rd to 8th rounds: As 2nd round.

9th round: 1 ch (does NOT count as st), 2 dc into first dc, 1 dc into each of next 7 dc, dc2tog over next 2 dc, 1 dc into next dc, dc2tog over next 2 dc, 1 dc into each of next 7 dc, 2 dc into last dc, ss to first dc, turn. 21 sts.

10th round: As 2nd round.

Fasten off.

SECOND LEG: Work as given for First Leg to end of 10th round.

Do NOT fasten off.

JOIN LEGS

11th round (RS): 1 ch (does NOT count as st), work 1 dc into each dc of Second Leg, then work 1 dc into each dc of First Leg, ss to first dc, turn. 42 sts.

Note: Where Legs join, small hole is formed. It will be much easier to sew this hole closed now.

12th round: 1 ch (does NOT count as st), dc2tog over first 2 dc, 1 dc into each of next 17 dc, (dc2tog over next 2 dc) twice, 1 dc into each of next 17 dc, dc2tog over next 2 dc, ss to first dc, turn. 38 sts.

13th round: 1 ch (does NOT count as st), dc2tog over first 2 dc, 1 dc into each of next 15 dc, (dc2tog over next 2 dc) twice, 1 dc into each of next 15 dc, dc2tog over next 2 dc, ss to first dc, turn. 34 sts.

14th to 19th rounds: As 2nd round.

20th round: 1 ch (does NOT count as st), (dc2tog over next 2 dc, 1 dc into each of next 4 dc, dc2tog over next 2 dc, 1 dc into next dc, dc2tog over next 2 dc, 1 dc into each of next 4 dc, dc2tog over next 2 dc) twice, ss to first dc, turn. 26 sts.

21st round: As 2nd round.

Fasten off.

Girl's skirt

With 3.5 mm hook and red, make 60 ch and join with a ss to form a ring.

1st round (RS): 1 ch (does NOT count as st), 1 dc into each ch to end, ss to first dc, turn. 60 sts.

2nd round: 1 ch (does NOT count as st), 1 dc into each dc to end, ss to first dc, turn.

3rd round: 1 ch (does NOT count as st), (1 dc into each of next 4 dc, dc2tog over next 2 dc, 1 dc into each of next 4 dc) 6 times, ss to first dc, turn. 54 sts.

4th to 6th rounds: As 2nd round.

7th round: 1 ch (does NOT count as st), (1 dc into each of next 3 dc, dc2tog over next 2 dc, 1 dc into each of next 4 dc) 6 times, ss to first dc, turn. 48 sts.

8th to 10th rounds: As 2nd round.

11th round: 1 ch (does NOT count as st), (1 dc into each of next 3 dc, dc2tog over next 2 dc, 1 dc into each of next 3 dc) 6 times, ss to first dc, turn. 42 sts.

12th and 13th rounds: As 2nd round.

14th round: 1 ch (does NOT count as st), (1 dc into each of next 2 dc, dc2tog over next 2 dc, 1 dc into each of next 3 dc) 6 times, ss to first dc, turn. 36 sts.

15th and 16th rounds: As 2nd round.

17th round: 1 ch (does NOT count as st), (1 dc into each of next 2 dc, dc2tog over next 2 dc, 1 dc into each of next 2 dc) 6 times, ss to first dc, turn. 30 sts.

18th and 19th rounds: As 2nd round.

20th round: 1 ch (does NOT count as st), (1 dc into next dc, dc2tog over next 2 dc, 1 dc into each of next 2 dc) 6 times, ss to first dc, turn. 24 sts.

21st round: As 2nd round.

Fasten off.

Using photograph as a guide, embroider lines of chain stitch around lower edge of skirt in navy and green.

Boy's sweater

SLEEVES

With 3.5 mm hook and red, make 14 ch and join with a ss to form a ring.

1st round (RS): 1 ch (does NOT count as st), 1 dc into each ch to end, ss to first dc, turn. 14 sts.

2nd round: 1 ch (does NOT count as st), 1 dc into each dc to end, ss to first dc, turn.

Join in green.

Working next 2 rounds using green, then continuing in stripes of 2 rounds in each colour, cont as follows:

3rd to 10th rounds: As 2nd round. Fasten off.

BODY

With 3.5 mm hook and green, make 32 ch and join with a ss to form a ring.

1st round (RS): 1 ch (does NOT count as st), 1 dc into each ch to end, ss to first dc, turn. 32 sts.

2nd round: 1 ch (does NOT count as st), 1 dc into each dc to end, ss to first dc, turn.

Join in red.

Working next 2 rounds using red, then continuing in stripes of 2 rounds in each colour, cont as follows:

3rd to 5th rounds: As 2nd round.

6th round: 1 ch (does NOT count as st), 1 dc into each of first 6 dc, (dc2tog over next 2 dc) twice, 1 dc into each of next 12 dc, (dc2tog over next 2 dc) twice, 1 dc into each of last 6 dc, ss to first dc, turn. 28 sts.

7th and 8th rounds: As 2nd round.

JOIN SLEEVES TO BODY

Keeping stripes correct and now working in rows, not rounds, cont as follows:

1st row (RS): 1 ch (does NOT count as st), 1 dc into each of first 5 dc of Body, dc2tog over next 2 dc, work around 14 dc of first Sleeve as follows: *dc2tog over first 2 dc, 1 dc into each of next 10 dc, dc2tog over last 2 dc*, work across next 14 dc of Body as follows: dc2tog over next 2 dc, 1 dc into each of next 10 dc, dc2tog over next 2 dc, work around 14 dc of second Sleeve in same way as for first Sleeve (by working from * to *), then work across rem 7 dc of Body as follows: dc2tog over next 2 dc, 1 dc into each of last 5 dc, turn. 48 sts.

Note: Where Sleeves join Body, small holes are formed at underarm. It will be much easier to sew these holes closed now.

2nd row: 1 ch (does NOT count as st), * 1 dc into each of next 4 dc, (dc2tog over next 2 dc) twice, 1 dc into each of next 8 dc, (dc2tog over next 2 dc) twice, 1 dc into each of next 4 dc, rep from * once more, turn. 40 sts.

3rd row: 1 ch (does NOT count as st), (1 dc into each of next 5 dc, dc2tog over next 2 dc, 1 dc into each of next 6 dc, dc2tog over next 2 dc, 1 dc into each of next 5 dc) twice, turn. 36 sts.

4th row: 1 ch (does NOT count as st), (1 dc into each of next 5 dc, dc2tog over next 2 dc, 1 dc into each of next 4 dc, dc2tog over next 2 dc, 1 dc into each of next 5 dc) twice, turn. 32 sts.

5th row: 1 ch (does NOT count as st), (1 dc into each of next 5 dc, dc2tog over next 2 dc, 1 dc into each of next 2 dc, dc2tog over next 2 dc, 1 dc into each of next 5 dc) twice, turn. 28 sts.

6th row: 1 ch (does NOT count as st), *1 dc into each of next 5 dc, (dc2tog over next 2 dc) twice, 1 dc into each of next 5 dc, rep from * once more, turn. 24 sts.

7th row: 1 ch (does NOT count as st), (1 dc into each of next 5 dc, dc2tog over next 2 dc, 1 dc into each of next 5 dc) twice, turn. 22 sts.

8th row: 1 ch (does NOT count as st), (1 dc into each of next 3 dc, dc2tog over next 2 dc, 1 dc into next dc, dc2tog over next 2 dc, 1 dc into each of next 3 dc) twice, turn. 18 sts.

Do NOT fasten off but slip working loop onto a safety pin.

Put Sweater onto Doll, slip hook back into working loop and close back neck opening by working ss to first dc, fasten off.

Girl's sweater

Work as given for Boy's Sweater but using green throughout.

Index

Yarn suppliers

ROWAN
Green Lane Mill
Holmfirth
West Yorks HD9 2DX
Tel: 44 (0)1484 681881
www.knitrowan.com
For international stockists see
website.

COLINETTE YARNS LTD
Banwy Workshops
Llanfair Caereinion
SY21 0SG
Powys
Wales
UK
Tel: 44 (0)1938 810128
Fax: 44 (0)1938 810127
www.colinette.com

TWILLEYS OF STAMFORD
Thomas B Ramsden & Co
   (Bradford) Ltd
Netherfield Road
Guiseley
Leeds LS20 9PD
Tel: 01943 872264
enquiries@tbramsden.co.uk
www.tbramsden.co.uk